friends

Geoff Baker

friends

Making and *keeping* them in today's busy world

inter-varsity press

INTER-VARSITY PRESS
38 De Montfort Street, Leicester LE1 7GP, England

© Geoff Baker 1999

First published 1999

British Library Cataloguing in Publication Data
A catalogue record for this book is available from the
British Library.

ISBN 0–85111–249–8

Set in Garamond
Printed in Great Britain

Inter-Varsity Press is the book-publishing division of the Universities and Colleges Christian Fellowship (formerly the Inter-Varsity Fellowship), a student movement linking Christian Unions in universities and colleges in the United Kingdom, and a member movement of the International Fellowship of Evangelical Students. For information about local and national activities write to UCCF, 38 De Montfort Street, Leicester LE1 7GP.

To Jo
with deepest love,
appreciation
and respect

Contents

Preface 9

Introduction:
Friendship against the odds 13

1 In the beginning 21

2 The enemy's strategy 29

3 What to look for in friendship 41

4 Choosing wisely 53

5 Back to reality 63

6 Celebrate the differences 73

7 A safe pair of hands 81

8 Breaking down the barriers 89

9 Tough love 101

10 Water in the desert 109

11 The family business 121

12 The offer of hope 131

13 When the going gets tough 143

14 Friendship and gender 153

Conclusion: A high-risk,
high-yield investment 165

Notes 173

Preface

Slumped in the chair opposite, Steve poured out his story. A once successful businessman, he had recently fallen victim to the recession. Now unemployed, struggling at his local church and raw from a broken relationship, he was desperately low. Just a few days later, Kathy sat in the same chair, tears streaming down her face, as she brought us up to date with her troubles. With three demanding children, a stormy relationship with her work-aholic husband and a growing overdraft, she was seriously depressed.

Their background and circumstances were very different, but they identified the same root cause of despair – loneliness. It was not their situation that made life seem unbearable so much as the sense of isolation within it. Kathy's predicament reminds us too that loneliness can strike someone constantly surrounded by people – even the closest family.

Several years have passed since those conversations, and both Steve and Kathy have come through their dark times.

Steve is once more employed and settled in a church, and is happily married; Kathy's situation is little changed. But both are largely restored to emotional and spiritual health. Many elements have been involved in that restoration, but both Steve and Kathy are sure about the key to their road back: friendship. They had friends who stuck by them when they were not much fun to know, and showed them God's love when they could not feel it for themselves: friends who loved them for who they were, and gave them a glimpse of who they could be.

Not long after this renaissance, we who had tried to care and support them were going through our own dark time, suffering from exhaustion and finding it hard to face the world. My wife Jo and I felt we had nothing more to give. I was finding it difficult to cope with people, and Jo was carrying the even greater load that my struggles brought with it.

The 'doctor' had become the 'patient' – but through God's grace the 'patient' had become the 'doctor' too. Steve's support and understanding were a vital part of our recovery process. His wise prayers, timely phone calls and unconditional love were of inestimable value. Kathy's kind and humorous gifts, her ability to make us laugh when we wanted to cry and her total acceptance of us in all our weakness helped to bring warmth and healing.

As we and they look back, we can see God's hand at work powerfully during those difficult times, let there be no mistake – but he chose to use fragile people as his hands and feet. It is difficult to overestimate the value of friendship in our walk with God. That is not to make us lose sight of our responsibility for a personal relationship with him, but to acknowledge that we were designed to work that out in the context of our relationships with others. We need friends, and in the giving and receiving of friendship as God intended it, there are riches to be found that grow in value the deeper we go.

Over the past few years I have become increasingly convinced that Christians need friendship more than ever, and work for it less than ever. The reasons are various and interconnected. Trends in our society take us away from community and towards insularity; time pressures mean that our stated priorities are difficult to work out practically; our fallen nature inclines us to pride and self-ishness, placing further obstacles in the path of developing good friendships.

As we look at these and other issues, and our response to them, I hope that the following pages will convince you too that there is every reason to work at building quality relationships. It's a costly business – a high-risk invest-ment, but a high-yield one too. Take the risk, and it might just revolutionize your understanding of friendship!

*The world's greatest tragedy is unwantedness;
the world's greatest disease is loneliness.*

Mother Theresa

*The LORD God said, 'It is not good for the
man to be alone.'*

Genesis 2:18

Introduction
Friendship against the odds

What Mother Theresa called the 'disease' of loneliness is turning into an epidemic. It has no regard for race, class or sex, and is a universal source of human suffering. Sociologist Robert Weiss, basing his thinking on a key study of loneliness in the early 1970s, estimated that 25% of the American population felt extremely lonely at some time during any given month.[1] This trend has worsened in the years since the study, and what is true for America is equally valid for Britain today. There is a well-documented link between loneliness and mental-health disorders, depression and even suicide, yet the trend towards greater isolation continues. The following factors certainly play their part.

People on the move

Gone are the days when it was the norm for someone to grow up, find work, marry, raise a family and stay in one place for a lifetime. Increased mobility, the job market and attitudes to career and employment have all contributed to the fragmentation of families and communities. People move to where the jobs are, or to enhance their career. Companies expect their employees to relocate, often seeing inflexibility as a sign of disloyalty or lack of commitment to the job.

This has a huge effect on our relationships. It is increasingly difficult to benefit from the support of the extended family, as they may live hundreds of miles away. Childhood friendships rarely survive the frequent changes of circumstance, and we view new relationships with caution. After all, we may be moving on again soon, and the closer our friendships become, the more painful the separation will be. It is easier to keep things on a more superficial level, and so avoid the potential heartache.

As for a sense of community, we are doing well if we even see our neighbours most days. Many houses are empty all day, and evenings and weekends are taken up, among other things, with trying to maintain the relationships that we already have in the limited time available.

Fear and cynicism

The pervading atmosphere in our society is certainly not conducive to friendship. The effects of the media on our thinking, and the problems of growing urbanization, have combined to create a mood of fear, cynicism and suspicion.

The role and influence of the media have increased considerably in the last decade. We have been taught to question everything we see and hear, often with good reason. Under ever closer scrutiny, many of our role models have been shown to have feet of clay. Whether in the realm of politics, religion, sport or entertainment, we have grown accustomed to the exposure of deceit and hypocrisy. It is little wonder that we find it increasingly difficult to take people at face value.

Added to this, the so-called inner-city problems of crime, violence and substance abuse are becoming increasingly obvious outside their acknowledged urban domain. It is no longer simply late at night and in certain places that we fear for our safety. As a reaction to these hazards we can find ourselves withdrawing from potentially dangerous proximity with strangers, as well as from the noise and commotion of urban life. The very act that protects us from others can, however, also bring a further sense of isolation and loneliness.

The leisure culture

There has been a huge growth in the 'leisure industry' during the last decade. The arts, sport and fitness, specialist hobbies and even (perhaps especially) shopping all fall into the category of leisure activities. Many have been quick to see and exploit the commercial possibilities of our preoccupation with amusement and recreation, offering ever more diverse, stimulating and bizarre ways to wile away our free time. The world is our oyster for the right price. It is all too easy to spend all our time in activity, and by default neglect the kind of conversation and companionship on which friendships can grow.

The most pervasive influence on our leisure time is still television. It disables communication in the home, and soaks up hour after hour. Some find it easier to live through actors on the screen than to interact with neighbours and relatives. With the greater choice that comes from satellite, cable and video, the opportunities to hide away from reality are almost endless. Whatever the benefits of television, it must be the number-one enemy of communication in our homes. Its capacity for impairing the growth of relationships is incalculable.

Technological development

The pace at which technology has progressed is staggering. This is especially obvious in computing and telecommunication. For an astonishingly low price, relatively speaking, we can purchase equipment which enables us to send or receive information in diverse forms almost anywhere in the world. These advancements have undoubtedly been a great boon to clearer, faster communication. We can keep in contact by mobile phone when on the move; we can fax or e-mail information instantly and directly. The social and business benefits are clear for all to see, but they are not without their price.

Phone, fax and e-mail all remove us one step from personal contact. The more efficient and effective they become, the more we rely on them and the less we actually relate face to face. It is hard for any relationship to grow beyond a certain level when conducted through an intermediary. Look, touch and facial expression are vital ingredients that we forgo. Whatever immediacy our technological advancements give us, we will never have complete relationships without contact.

The Christian sub-culture

Further to the trends just highlighted, for most Christians there is also the core question of involvement in the life of the Christian community. This will probably mean attendance at a Christian Union, church or fellowship, house-group, prayer triplet or all of these. In addition, we may have specific responsibilities, with their own meetings, rehearsals or preparations, not to mention special events, conferences, concerts, celebrations and conventions. Church leaders can unintentionally place a huge burden of guilt on their members by equating attendance at all meetings with true commitment to the church and thus to Christ. Though there is a link in most cases, it is a far more complex equation than first appearances might suggest.

Sadly, in our desire to serve God in the context of our local Christian community, we can so easily find that our relationship with both him and others suffers. There are more meetings, more responsibilities and more activities, and consequently there is less time to form lasting friendships. In the place where we would look for the greatest depth and reality in our friends, time constraints push us to a kind of hearty superficiality. We are too busy 'doing' to 'be', and, even when we catch a glimpse of that truth, the merry-go-round of activity rarely slows down enough for us to get off.

The tendency away from relationships and community is by no means what people claim to want or need. Indeed, the eminent psychologist Abraham Maslow sums up the research and thinking of many with the observation that after food and shelter, the next basic human need is to engage in relationships.[2] So why the continuing drift towards loneliness? If we have such a desire and need to be in relationships, surely we would not sacrifice it so readily under the pressures I have outlined?

It is at this point that we have to acknowledge our fallen nature. The consequences of sin in our lives and in those around us mean that we are fighting not just against external trends, but against natural inclinations. These can't be dealt with by local or national government measures; they need the Holy Spirit's power in individual lives to bring conviction and change.

Because we are swimming against the tide of society, it will take time, effort and perseverance, but it is vital to invest in our relationships. The battle for friendship is on, and with God's help we will win.

He wanted friendship
and they offered him friendliness;
he wanted steak and they offered Spam.

Bernard Malamud

Chapter 1
In the beginning

In the beginning God was in relationship. Before humankind came into being, in the very act of creation there was partnership. God said, 'Let *us* make man in *our* image, in *our* likeness …' (Genesis 1:26). From before time, Father, Son and Holy Spirit were talking, working and resting in the most intimate and harmonious of relationships. And when God said, 'It is not good for the man to be alone' (Genesis 2:18), it had a significance far beyond the confines of marriage. We who are made in the image of God are designed to function properly in the context of relationships.

The Bible gives many examples of rich friendships, some of which flourished against all the odds. Ruth and Naomi bridged the gap between generations and cultures. Ruth was helped by Naomi's wisdom, and Naomi benefited from her daughter-in-law's faithfulness. David and Jonathan formed a friendship that overcame distance and family conflict, and whose effects were seen way beyond Jonathan's death in David's kindness to his crippled son. In the book of Acts, we see the friendship between Paul and Timothy develop; the apostle's letters to Timothy give further insight into his fatherly fondness for this young man, and the input he gives.

Close, committed friendship is one of the most fulfilling and productive forms of relationship, yet one that has been consistently neglected. As many people are seeing the damaging effects of individualism on our society, however, there is a growing awareness of the importance of friendship. This is reflected too in the growth of small groups within the church, as a basis for support, encouragement and growth.

What is friendship?

The classical philosophers, who placed a great deal of emphasis on the importance of friendship, came up with some helpful definitions which can provide a useful starting-point. Theologian David Westberg writes of Aristotle:

> In Aristotle's analysis, friendship is based on a relationship in which something is shared – that is its essence. There are three categories of friendship, two of which are inferior: 1. a friendship based on pleasure (two or more people enjoying the same activity); and 2. a friendship based on usefulness (as when neighbours or business associates derive mutual advantage from a relationship). 3. True friendship, however, is based on virtue, not profit or pleasure. Such friendship is found when one loves someone for the moral qualities he or she has, and desires good for that person.[1]

The tradition of the classical philosophers was assimilated into Christian thought, with certain distinctives. One of the most important was distinguishing between friendship for pleasure (worldly friendship) and a friendship based on true spirituality, which was guided by love rather than by selfish interests.

An important added dimension for Christians is the concept of *fellowship*. The New Testament Greek word *koinonia* means 'participation, sharing, communion with someone in something'. On a basic level that could apply to people who share a hobby, business partners, football teams and the like. From a Christian perspective, however, fellowship is a far deeper concept. It is not simply sharing a common interest, or striving towards a common objective. The basis of Christian fellowship is sharing in Christ.

By faith the believer enters into Christ's suffering, death and burial, and so, amazingly, can participate in his resurrection, ascension and glory.[2] Perhaps the most tangible expression of this fellowship occurs when we share in the bread and wine of communion. As we participate in the fellowship meal together, we are accepting one another as true participants in Christ.

Our fellowship with God in Christ by the power of the Spirit will inevitably lead to a deeper fellowship with other Christians. We join a community fuelled by love and forgiveness. The isolating effects of sin can be overcome, and we can enjoy the deepest of fellowship with God and with our fellow believers. Our relationships are further deepened by partnership in the gospel, giving us a common sense of purpose and direction. That is our ideal.

The reality is often a different matter entirely. In many churches, it has to be said, the concept of fellowship is actually more superficial than a friendship without any spiritual dimension. It has been reduced to fulfilling tasks, enduring recreational activities and drinking coffee together after the service. This is due partly to conflicts within and among ourselves, which prevent us enjoying true friendship enriched by fellowship.

Conflicts in church life

Spirituality and reality

We know we are supposed to be spiritual; after all, we are Christians. The problem is, we often have an unhelpful understanding of what spirituality is. It seems to involve quoting Bible verses and using words like 'blessed', 'share' and, yes, 'fellowship'. After the service, the conversation can feel like entering a parallel universe. We end up merely endorsing truth (God is good, faithful and in control, and we need to trust him) without applying it to our lives or circumstances. Such conversations are not so much bad as irrelevant. There is little connection between the way we express our spirituality and the reality of our experience. We are saying the right things, going through the motions, but certainly not building real relationships.

A healthier understanding of spirituality involves integrating our experiences, feelings and circumstances with our faith. Then in our friendships we can share in the process of applying biblical truth to our life and culture, instead of ignoring or denying these things. Our relationship with God can be worked out in the context of relationships with one another.

Image and substance

Some of us base our idea of fellowship on the notion that 'we are all good Christians'. 'We all have a lengthy time of prayer and Bible study each day. We all love everyone, and wouldn't dream of saying, doing or thinking anything bad. If there are problems, they are the type that we used to struggle with; we are never struggling with them right now. Of course, we are nothing like that at all, but it is quite clear that everyone else is, so we dare not admit our weaknesses.

Such flawed thinking creates an environment in which we keep each other at arm's length, in case anyone discovers what we are really like. Consequently, instead of being able to encourage one another towards Christlike living, we drift towards the isolation caused by fear. A hale and hearty camaraderie serves only to mask our superficiality. What we have is less than friendship, and nothing like fellowship.

Peter Meadows describes the ten minutes after a Sunday service as the 'Sunday lie-in', when conversations run something like this:

'Hello, Barbara, how are you?' (Must dash to get the lunch on.)

'Fine, Julie, fine' (except for three sleepless nights with baby James, a blazing row with Mike – again – and a panic attack at Sainsbury's). 'And how are you?'

'Fine.' (Thank goodness she doesn't know. She'd have a fit.) 'And you, Tom?'

'Fine. Just fine.' (If I told her even half, it would be round this place faster than headlice at a nursery school.) 'How are you, Stephen?'

'Oh, fine, really fine.' (If you really care, where have you been all week while life has been kicking me in the teeth?)[3]

Our dishonesty often stems from the misplaced desire to keep up appearances. The effort that goes into maintaining our image would be so much better spent on our substance. Unless we make inroads in this aspect of church life, the quality of our friendships will be severely limited. This goes for church leaders as well as for everyone else.

Programmes and people

'You can tell he's an out-and-out Christian,' the old joke goes, 'because when you call at his home, he's never there!' This is too true to be funny (as well as being an awful joke). In our worthy desire to learn Christian truth, serve God and enjoy the full riches of Christian community, we find ourselves in a never-ending cycle of activity. When we are not attending meetings, we are preparing, organizing, discussing and assessing. Even organizing fun events can be difficult, as we try to take account of everyone's needs and sensitivities.

All this leaves little time to develop friendships. We may well be working and talking together, but we tend to be discussing the matter in hand rather than issues in our lives. We become colleagues rather than friends. Activities become ends in themselves instead of means to an end. Our time and energies are hijacked by programmes, but it is people that are important.

Conflicts like these erode our understanding and practice of fellowship as God intended. In the very community where friendships could be at their deepest, we settle for a pale imitation of the real thing. How can we rediscover the true meaning of fellowship in our churches? The next chapter starts to answer this question by trying to identify where the root of the problem lies.

Think about …

- your relationships (including your relationship with God) and how deep or shallow each of them is
- activism and genuine fellowship in your church, and how you might begin to deal with the problem

Loneliness is a crowded room.

Bryan Ferry

The L*ORD* *is my rock, my fortress*
and my deliverer;
my God is my rock, in whom I take refuge.

Psalm 18:2

Chapter 2
The enemy's strategy

Many Christians, asked to list their priorities in life might mention such aims as these:

- developing a relationship with God
- nurturing quality relationships with family and friends
- providing for my needs and those of my family
- reaching out with the gospel into the wider community

Yet if the same people were observed over a period of time, to see what they invested most time, money and energy in, the list might look more like this:

- pursuing career advancement
- improving their family's standard of living
- enjoying social and leisure activities
- staying young, fit, out of debt and out of hospital

You might call the comparison harsh, cynical or exaggerated, but it does point to a contradiction between our theory and our practice. And the contradiction is only too apparent when it comes to friendship. There is a universal cry for deeper, more meaningful friendships and a common lament about loneliness, and yet at the same time the things that take our time and energy appear to lead us away from the very thing we crave so much.

Why do we live like this? We looked earlier at some of the social, cultural and circumstantial factors. But if these were the real causes surely we would have found practical solutions long ago? I must confess that the deeper my studies have gone in this area, the more convinced I have become that there are more questions than answers. That having been said, there are some fundamental biblical principles that give us a glimpse of what lies at the heart of our struggles. They can be found in Jesus' reply to an important question.

> One of them [the Pharisees], an expert in the law, tested him [Jesus] with this question: 'Teacher, which is the greatest commandment in the Law?'
> Jesus replied: '"Love the Lord your God with all your heart and with all your soul and with all your mind." This is the first and greatest commandment. And the second is like it: "Love your neighbour as yourself." All the Law and the Prophets hang on these two commandments' (Matthew 22:35–40).

Jesus' answer tells us something crucial about what God wants for his people. The expert is asking about commandments, rules; Jesus says the most important commandments point to love. Not only that, but all the other commandments depend on these two.

God's plan has always been that we should enjoy a

relationship with him, based on love; and that from that foundation we should reach out in relationships with those around us. It is not surprising that Satan's strategies so often strike at the heart of these crucial relationships. Satan wants to wreck our relationship with God, and spoil our earthly relationships.

From the beginning

The enemy strategy was in evidence from the beginning of the human race. Adam and Eve enjoyed a close relationship with God and with each other (Genesis 2). Then the serpent questioned what God had said, placing doubts in their minds and tempting them to rebellion and sin. With frightening speed the harmonious relationships were shattered. Adam and Eve hid from God, blamed others for their own actions and were banished from the Garden. Sin had brought with it a curse which affected all relationships (Genesis 3).

The consequences become dramatically evident in their two boys, Cain and Abel. When Cain's offering to God was not acceptable, he ignored God's warning instead of putting right what was wrong. His anger towards God and jealousy towards his brother culminated in the first murder. Cain was further alienated from others by his actions, and was left despairing at being hidden from God's presence, a restless wanderer on the earth (Genesis 4:13). The relationships he longed for and grieved over were the very ones that his own sin had spoiled.

The pattern continues throughout history. Friends and families are divided; nations war with other nations, and are divided themselves in civil wars; God's people are constantly being weakened by feuds and schisms. Fear, hostility and mistrust play an unwelcome part in all our lives. In such a climate, friendship is difficult and loneliness widespread.

Yesterday I travelled to London for yet another committee meeting. My journey highlighted these truths. On the train coats and bags were placed on seats to form physical barriers: 'Don't sit next to me!' Eye contact was avoided; eyes were closed, hidden behind a newspaper or staring blankly into a world inhabited by fantasies. Nobody speaks with a stranger.

At the station, patrolling police officers were a reminder that we are not all out to help each other. Tourists held their cameras and bags tightly, fearful of pickpockets. Commuters looked lost in their own thoughts. There was the noise of thousands of feet, and of occasional buskers, but very few voices.

Yet all around us on the advertising hoardings are images of happy, smiling men, women and children engaged in numerous activities that speak of friendship, intimacy, security and fulfilment. As I checked once more that my wallet was safe, I was deeply saddened by the contrast between our desires and our reality. At the root of our loneliness and isolation lies separation from our heavenly Father and from our fellow human beings.

Sin in our lives

We constantly face the temptation to put ourselves first, to do things our way, to make ourselves the ultimate reference point. The essence of sin is self. Even when we know what is right, we struggle with the mindset of the world, our own human nature and the sneak tactics of the enemy.

Pride

Our pride forms a barrier to openness and the development of friendships. It causes us to protect our reputation
to the detriment of our character, to elevate ourselves at
the expense of others and to focus on image while
neglecting substance. Pride refuses to let us allow others
close for fear of what they might discover.

It might take the form of refusing to admit our need or
weakness by asking for help or advice. It might incline us
to work far harder on our presentational and social skills
than we do on our attitude and motivation. We may be
tempted to look for position and kudos instead of the
opportunity to serve, and to take glory for ourselves that
belongs to God. The enemy uses pride in these ways to
drive a wedge between us and those we love.

Selfishness

Our selfishness damages the potential for good friendships
by warring against our desires to put others first. It
muddies the waters of our best intentions. Selfishness
hurts the very people we want to love.

How often our great plans for time with God and with
others are scuppered by subtle temptations! Another few
minutes in bed, another evening in front of the television,
another DIY project. We are so busy making our homes
into places people might enjoy visiting that we never
have time to invite them! Our preoccupation with self-
fulfilment, self-improvement and self-preservation steals
the time and energy that could reach out to others. The
enemy uses self-love and lack of self-discipline to keep us
from our relationships, no matter how loudly we proclaim
that they are our priority.

Rebellion

At the heart of our sin is rebellion against God. We don't want to do things his way. We battle with the temptation to circumvent his will, and with the inbred instinct that our wisdom is somehow comparable with his. Our rebellion causes us to look for answers outside God and his Word, to try to find external solutions for internal problems and to ask people to meet needs that only God can and should. The result is inevitably disappointment and frustration. Henri Nouwen's words are revealing:

> No friend or lover, no husband or wife, no community or commune will be able to put to rest our deepest cravings for unity and wholeness. And by burdening others with these divine expectations, of which we ourselves are only partially aware, we might inhibit the expression of free friendship and evoke instead feelings of inadequacy and weakness … It is sad to see how sometimes people suffering from loneliness, often deepened by the lack of affection in their intimate family circle, search for a final solution for their pains and look at a new friend, a new lover or a new community with Messianic expectations.[1]

That longing to find the heart's true home is in all of us, but the enemy sidetracks our search, tempting us to look in the wrong places for our solutions. Friendships are flawed by sin, and that ensures that they will never meet our ideals. The resulting disappointment will incline us to reject the opportunity to work at real, 'warts and all' friendships and move on to the next hope of perfection. We can end up permanently caught between the frustration of superficiality and the disappointment of reality.

At the heart of our security should be total dependence on God. At the heart of our self-esteem should be the knowledge that we are loved by God. It is from that bedrock alone that we can move out with confidence. Although friends can help to show us that love and security, they can never take the place of it.

Sin in the lives of others

If our own sin separates us *from* others, so does our response to the sin we encounter *in* others. The defence mechanisms we employ make it increasingly difficult to form meaningful friendships. Greed and violence in our society engender fear and hostility. We feel the need to protect ourselves, and the physical barriers that protect us from harm also keep out those who would bring good. The selfishness in all of us creates an environment of mutual mistrust. Nouwen comments:

> In our world the assumption is that strangers are a potential danger and that it is up to them to disprove it ... Our heart might desire to help others; to feed the hungry, visit the prisoners and offer shelter to travellers; but meanwhile we have surrounded ourselves with a wall of hostile feelings, instinctively avoiding people and places where we might be reminded of our good intentions.[2]

Such fear and hostility are by no means limited to our encounters with strangers. Even with those close to us — work colleagues, classmates, team-mates — there can be fear and hostility. When there are threats, whether perceived or real, to our standing or security, loyalty and friendship are often the first victims. Sadly, petty rivalry and jealousy have spilled over into even the caring professions.

Our natural response is to protect ourselves from pain. Letting people come close gives them the opportunity to hurt us, so we keep them at a distance. We can be surrounded by people, part of the Christian community even, never alone but deeply lonely. The sin in our lives and our world has done its job, wrecking our relationship with God, and spoiling our earthly relationships.

Reaching out

If the history of the human race is in part the tragic story of Satan's efforts to bring separation, it is far more importantly the wonderful story of God reaching out, down the ages, to bring reconciliation. The culmination is found in Jesus, the Prince of Peace. In Luke's account of the events surrounding Jesus' birth, a host of angels appear to some shepherds. Their words are significant: 'Glory to God in the highest, and on earth peace to men on whom his favour rests' (Luke 2:14). From the outset, those twin themes of relationship with God and with humankind were evident; God desired to show his love, and to see people enjoy harmonious relationships. Peace with one another would grow out of peace with God.

The apostle Paul tells of God 'reconciling the world to himself in Christ, not counting men's sins against them'. He goes on to explain how that was achieved: 'God made him who had no sin to be sin for us, so that in him we might become the righteousness of God' (2 Corinthians 5:19, 21). Jesus' death on the cross, taking our punishment on himself, paid the price for our sin and cleared the way for forgiveness and a restored relationship with God. Much of the New Testament helps us understand how we can maintain and develop that relationship, with the Holy Spirit's power, and how we can do the same in our human relationships.

So the pieces are in place to combat the enemy strategy. Jesus has provided forgiveness and a restored relationship with God. The Holy Spirit gives us power to change. The Bible lays down guidelines for building right relationships. Our Christianity, then, should make us far better friends.

But we need to be alert, for the enemy will continue to tempt, and our sinful nature will continue to resurface. Pride, selfishness and rebellion are never far away, and we will need to make a conscious effort to combat them with the Holy Spirit's help. Sin in the lives of others will continue to bring feelings of fear and hostility, and we will need to fight our natural instincts to draw back, choosing instead to reach out beyond our comfort zones.

Understanding what lies at the heart of those struggles which push us towards loneliness will help protect us from Satan's strategies. Being honest about our natural inclinations will save us from making superficial judgments on failures in friendship. Knowing God's heart and will for us will prompt us to keep reaching out through our pride and fear to be part of his master plan of reconciliation.

With God's help we can face up to the huge gap between our theoretical priorities and our practical ones, and with the Spirit's power we can begin to close that gap. Each time we choose to reach out we frustrate the enemy's plans and, even more importantly, do what God loves. That reaching out will involve a commitment to expressions of openness and humility, and to acts of kindness and service. It will mean taking firm action with our diaries to give time to what our stated priorities are. It will mean having the courage to progress beyond hostility to hospitality. That may seem daunting, but eventually we may be amazed to discover how many valued friendships began with a simple act of reaching out.

Think about ...

- identifying which particular sin makes which friendships more difficult for you
- people you know, to whom you could start to reach out in friendship
- finding ways to treat strangers with hospitality, not hostility

The only reward of virtue is virtue;
the only way to have a friend is to be one.

Ralph Waldo Emerson

Chapter 3
What to look for in friendship

Two are better than one,
   because they have a good return for their
   work:
If one falls down,
   his friend can help him up.
But pity the man who falls
   and has no-one to help him up!
Also, if two lie down together, they will keep
   warm.
   But how can one keep warm alone?
Though one may be overpowered,
   two can defend themselves.
A cord of three strands is not quickly broken.

(Ecclesiastes 4:9–12)

What exactly should we be looking for in true friendship? Of course, whatever we hope to receive from it, we should be prepared to give. Without that underlying attitude, we will always struggle to maintain good friendships. Here are some key areas where friends can give and receive.

Effectiveness

> Two are better than one,
>   because they have a good return for their work.

If you have ever had to put together a piece of self-assembly furniture, you will understand the truth of the above statement. Working solo, it can take for ever. The diagrams are often unclear, the instructions are baffling and the task requires astonishing manual dexterity or, failing that, three arms. Working together, however, the job is done in half the time. There are two pairs of hands to fix things together; there are two minds to puzzle out how it should be done.

This works only if there is true unity of purpose. You may have experienced the nightmare of working on a project with someone who wants to tackle it in quite a different way from you. Then it takes twice as long! Stubborness, inflexibility and poor communication reduce effectiveness. The four hands and two minds need a commitment to work together, with care, consideration and compromise.

As we encounter the problems and opportunities of everyday life, the same principle holds true. Our ability to make the best of our circumstances is greatly increased by having hearts, minds and hands united in friendship, with a common purpose. On some occasions this unity will express itself in practical ways, and on others in deeply spiritual ones. What is vital is a commitment to work together, to join forces in a way that takes us beyond personal preference and comfort. We will bring our strengths to the relationship, and recognize our weaknesses. We will bring our perspectives, and acknowledge the validity of our friend's viewpoint. We will be willing to help even if it is not on our terms. In that environment, friendships will be increasingly effective and productive, and individuals will grow.

In recent months our church has taken on another staff member to work alongside me. The workload had grown beyond manageable proportions, and so an extra person was badly needed – but Richard brings far more than a division of labour. As we share our hopes and vision for the future, we are both encouraged and motivated. As we mull over problems together, one or the other always seems to find the key that unlocks the solution. As we pool our ideas, they are shaped and developed way beyond what was originally envisaged. We work more than twice as fast, achieve more than twice as much, and do each other good into the bargain. We are far more than colleagues; we are friends, and as we work together we produce a better return on our work. We are more effective, more productive, more fulfilled through our partnership.

If we are finding that two are *not* better than one, we have some serious questions to ask of our friendships, marriages and partnerships. In our search to build better relationships, this is a vital truth: we need to give in such a way that our joint effectiveness is greatly increased. We look for those who are prepared to do the same. Two *are* better than one. If that is what we believe and want, and are committed to, then that will be our experience.

Support

> If one falls down,
>   his friend can help him up.
> But pity the man who falls
>   and has no-one to help him up!

All of us have suffered the pain of a fall at some time. We stumble or slip, take a quick look to see if anyone has noticed, and walk on nonchalantly, trying to regain our composure. All that has been hurt is our pride. A more severe fall, however, dents more than our dignity. We can be severely shaken, confused and disorientated, and seriously injured. How grateful we are when friends pick us up, dust us off and help us to recover – and how conscious we are of being alone when they are not there! If pride keeps us from accepting their assistance, we are foolish indeed.

Mostly we fall down in ways other than physical. Temptation leads to sin; ignorance to error; pride to humiliation. We fall foul of circumstances through no fault of our own. Hasty and unwise choices bring unforeseen and unwelcome consequences. Falls of this sort set the same feelings rushing over us. At best, our pride is hurt; at worst, we are shaken, confused, disorientated and hurting inside. It is at such times that good friends are worth their weight in gold: friends who will pick us up and comfort us; who will help us to resolve the problems and bring healing where there is pain; friends who are more concerned with seeing us on our feet again than with pointing out the stupidity of our fall.

But helping friends isn't always that easy. They may be too ashamed or embarrassed to let us know their need. They may be too proud to consider asking for help. They may compound the problem by rejecting our offers, determined to go it alone despite their sorry predicament. And that is where true friends will need to go beyond the initial rejection and keep on offering their hand. A combination of tough skin and a soft heart is very helpful in such situations.

Friends are committed to picking us up when we fall, even if their help isn't always appreciated.

Some time before my colleague Richard's arrival, the combined pressures of a rapidly growing young church (which was engaged in a building programme), a large number of outside engagements and a young family were taking their toll. I couldn't sleep, suffered anxiety attacks and was likely to break down in tears for no discernible reason. Only my wife Jo knew the full extent of the problem, and took the brunt of it with exemplary grace and love. But still I carried on, saying the right things, smiling the right smiles, doing the things a minister is supposed to do.

It wasn't until a friend on the leadership team came round one evening that things came to a head. Jo wouldn't let me hide the problem any more, and Paul took matters into his own hands. 'You have to stop immediately,' he said.

'But who's going to …?' That was about as far as I got. That evening Paul began the process that gave me a vital period of rest, and the sense of relief was enormous.

Paul wasn't the first to ask questions. Jo had been giving helpful advice and input, and other friends had expressed concern. Why was I prepared to ignore it all, to put my health at risk and my family under pressure, and potentially to leave the church without a minister? It may have been due partly to a sense of responsibility, and partly to being unable to think clearly. But I have to admit that pride was a major factor. After all, wasn't I the one who was supposed to have the answers, solve others' problems and always be strong? And who would do the job properly if I didn't do it? It was all very well telling others they had nothing to be ashamed of or embarrassed about in asking for help with their struggles; I was decidedly embarrassed about my own inability to cope. My pride had kept me from asking for help or receiving it when it was offered.

We who have fallen have a responsibility too. If we accept that true friends are pledged to help each other when they fall, then we must be prepared, to admit our need and ask for help. A dent to our pride is a small price to pay for help, and without the humility to admit our need our friendships will always lack a vital dimension.

When we cannot walk unaided, friends are there to lean on. The joy of experiencing such support is matched only by the pleasure of giving it. True friends will provide that sort of support for each other, persevering beyond initial rejection. True friends will be open and prepared to receive it, setting aside their pride and shame.

Comfort and companionship

Also, if two lie down together, they will keep warm.
But how can one keep warm alone?

Clearly the initial picture intended here is of a marriage relationship, but the need for warmth, comfort and companionship extends far beyond the marital bed. The physical warmth that would have been so crucial in the days before central heating has its emotional and spiritual counterparts too. We rarely lack the means of physical warmth; the same cannot always be said of us emotionally and spiritually.

Picture a cosy evening in front of the fire. The friends have shared so much more than the warmth of a fire. A lovely meal, and conversation full of generosity and humour, has helped them to relax thoroughly. Coffee and a favourite CD create the background for more reflective talk, when they can share more intimate thoughts. At the end of the evening they feel loved and accepted, strengthened in their faith and better prepared to face tomorrow.

This is a depth of friendship that can be achieved only with small numbers. Most of us have known what it is like to feel alone in a crowd, for we need so much more than the proximity of people. That is one of the reasons church meetings alone will never meet the needs of the lonely. Good friendships can provide the comfort and companionship that are crucial to our well-being.

Sadly, families can often become increasingly insular. While enjoying their own warmth and security, they neglect to share those benefits with others. For many single people, their only glimpse of family life is the ten-minute gap between their arrival to babysit and the couple's departure for their evening out.

One simple way of enriching friendships is for families to open their home beyond set-piece occasions. Sharing mealtimes, children's bathtimes and bedtimes; allowing others to enter into the warmth and fun of family life – this can have enormous benefits on both sides. Children benefit greatly from positive contact with other adults; parents are taken out of what can become a mind-numbing routine; single friends are able to enjoy family closeness and warm contact with the opposite sex in a secure and protected environment.

Whether single or married, the way we use our homes can make a huge difference to the quality of our friendships. People whose style is formal and whose home is unwelcoming will find it difficult to develop relationships that warm the heart. Warm, open homes create the environment in which warm, open friendships flourish. Look for friends like that, and look to be a friend like that.

Protection

> Though one may be overpowered,
> two can defend themselves.

The picture changes abruptly from a cosy home to an open road. We are taken back two or three thousand years to the kind of journey that regularly took place between towns. At night, there was the danger of wild beasts; in the day, rocks might hide opportunist bandits, only too willing to relieve travellers of their worldly goods. Walking a road like that, travellers really appreciated the value of a friend, especially one with a keen eye and a strong arm.

Thankfully, our everyday journeys do not present these hazards. On our journey of life and faith, however, there is a constant danger of ambush. Our main sources of attack are that unholy trinity, the world, the flesh and the devil. We find our thinking overpowered by the world and our desires by the flesh. Behind these temptations we see the work of the devil. The attacks often come when we are at our most vulnerable, or expecting them the least.

Understanding that truth serves to emphasize the need for good companions on our journey: friends with keen spiritual eyesight, who can spot a potential ambush; friends who are looking out for us; who are prepared to ask hard questions and say uncomfortable things in order to protect us from sin and failure; friends who will stand with us in the heat of the battle, praying, loving and pointing us to our salvation in Christ.

A key aspect of friendship is being a trusted travelling companion on the spiritual journey. That is the sort of friend we need: someone who helps to keep us from danger and who won't desert us when things get tough. That is the sort of friend we should seek to be.

Strength

A cord of three strands is not quickly broken.

Our final picture is of a rope made up of three strands intertwined. The third strand, so I'm told, gives a far greater strength to the rope than we would imagine. One strand is weak, two strands are a considerable improvement, but three strands are, well, pretty impressive.

The move from two to three is significant, for many friendships are weakened by excluding other people. That is often true in the case of marriage. Our partners are our best friends; this is as it should be, but it is not enough. Couples are often too close to each other to be objective, and both parties would benefit hugely from an outside perspective. Some subjects are simply ignored because they always cause friction, and yet they badly need to be addressed. A third party could help that to happen without matters getting too emotive or breaking down into the usual arguments. Of course, such situations need to be handled with wisdom and caution.

There is also a great strength in same-sex friendships which marriage cannot provide. We will be examining this further in a later chapter; suffice it to say here that we can communicate on a different level with members of the same sex and that this can be very helpful.

It is not only marriage partners that shut out other people. Wherever it might arise, the principle remains the same: there is great benefit in broadening our base of friendship. Different perspectives, gifts and strengths are immensely enriching. During difficult times, when we need to lean on others, the burden can be shared and the level of support maintained.

With friendship there is undoubtedly great strength in depth, but it isn't simply a case of 'the more the merrier'. If we try to broaden our base too much, we will find it hard to sustain any meaningful level of friendship. There is no optimum number for all, for our circumstances differ enormously. We simply need to be realistic, and not confuse quality with quantity.

Increased effectiveness, support, comfort and companionship, protection, strength: these are qualities we look for in friendship; these are qualities we try to bring to friendship.

Think about ...

- qualities to look for in friendship
- qualities to bring to friendship
- what to do to build your friendships on a stronger basis

He who walks with the wise grows wise,
but a companion of fools suffers harm.

Proverbs 13:20

Bad company corrupts good character.

1 Corinthians 15:33

Perfume and incense bring joy to the heart,
and the pleasantness of one's friend springs
from his earnest counsel.

Proverbs 27:9

Chapter 4
Choosing wisely

We do not choose our friends like items from a super-market shelf: 'You look like a splendid sort of individual; let's be friends!' Building a friendship is an intricate process, taking into account our needs, the needs of others, and the circumstances we find ourselves in.

Maybe a few of your friends are people you might never have chosen or expected to have as friends. You met when they were having a bad time, and you were able to offer support and encouragement. Although currently they bring little and receive much, that is not an issue. Giving to those from whom we expect little in return is part of our Christian calling. One day the situation may well be reversed, and we shall be grateful for their support. Some of your friends might never have chosen you either, but you needed their help and they were open and generous to you.

Other friendships grow out of circumstances. Similar interests, children of the same age, shared struggles – these are some of the elements that can form the initial bond.

Those who live in small villages may find there is only one other person of a similar age, so circumstances throw them together. They may not have chosen the relationship in an ideal world, but it is a far better option than solitude.

Nevertheless, there remains a strong element of choice in the process of building friendships.

Givers or takers?

In his book *Restoring your Spiritual Passion*, Gordon MacDonald reminds us of the effect those around us have on us:

> I can think of certain people in my world whose company invigorates me, and when they leave, I am full of resolve, ideas, and intentions about God, self-improvement, and service to others. I can think of other people in my world whose presence exhausts me. And when they leave, I am ready for a long, long nap. An old friend of mine used to say of people, 'Some folk bring joy wherever they go; others bring joy *when* they go.' We need to understand the people of our world and how they play a part in the potential invigoration or weariness of our lives.[1]

MacDonald's words strike a chord. Only this week I have spent two hours that felt like ten with someone who grabs every waking hour offered, and then comes back for more. This person moves from one crisis to the next, soaks up encouragement like blotting paper and constantly returns to issues that have supposedly been dealt with long ago. Our counselling sessions leave me drained and unable to complete the remaining tasks for the day. Then perhaps the phone rings; I answer with trepidation, but it is a dear friend calling to see how things are going. The call lasts less than ten minutes, but I put the phone down smiling, feeling refreshed, encouraged and ready to face the rest of the day.

MacDonald divides people into five categories: (1) the Very Resourceful People, who ignite our passion; (2) the Very Important People, who share our passion; (3) the Very Trainable People, who catch our passion; (4) the Very Nice People, who enjoy our passion; and (5) the Very Draining People, who sap our passion. People in the first two groups give us vital input, and those in the third take effort, but with positive consequences. Those in groups 4 and 5, however, can take all our time and energy, leaving us drained and unable to help anyone effectively. MacDonald continues:

> But even more significantly, by spending my prime time with these two groups, I was expending my own energy in nonrestorable ways. Every minute of that time was a one-way flow of passion (outward), sometimes necessary (as in the case of the woman who touched Jesus' robe) but, in the long run, seriously debilitating.
>
> We grow weary when we do not learn this lesson in time. I have watched many laypeople quit responsibilities, even become embittered over church activity, because no-one taught them how to protect themselves from draining people.[2]

Draining people are part of the fellowship of believers. We should minister to them; they will form part of our network of friends. But it is important to spend significant time with those who can give input, and bring us spiritual refreshment and energy. Without that we will lose our vitality and may well become discouraged and bitter. The end result could be disastrous. We will certainly be in no position to help others when we have no resources left ourselves. Making wise choices about friendships will involve finding a balance between the givers and the takers, and giving due regard to our own needs.

Friend or foe?

> It is better to heed a wise man's rebuke
> than to listen to the song of fools.

> (Ecclesiastes 7:5)

Which would you rather have: a rebuke or a compliment? For me, it depends from whose lips it comes. A rebuke from someone who loves me and has insight into my life is infinitely more valuable than praise from someone who knows me superficially. But praise is nice! It makes me feel good, lifts my spirits and encourages me; and what could be wrong with that? The writer of Ecclesiastes makes the point that it doesn't matter how charming the song is; if the words are rooted in foolishness, they will do the hearer no good at all. In fact they may do harm, for false praise is dangerous.

Insincere praise is flattery, and flattery can be harmful. Sometimes it is offered from the best of motives, by those who are trying to be nice, kind and encouraging. At other times the motives are not so pure. The flatterer pays a compliment in the hope that he or she might get a return on it. Either way, flatterers set people up for failure and disappointment. 'Whoever flatters a neighbour is spreading a net for his feet' (Proverbs 29:5). Flattery can trap us, trip us up and cause us to fall. In his book *That's Not What I Meant*, Tim Stafford gives a good example of that process.

> I know a man who sincerely felt a very strong call from God to full-time Christian ministry. He decided to go to Bible school to train as a pastor. He was not a good student, and the course work and expense put a great strain on him and his family. But he persevered and got his degree. He then found out what anyone who really knew him might have predicted; that no church, however small and struggling, would call him to be their pastor.
>
> He was a wonderful fellow with a great heart, but he utterly lacked the kind of leadership ability that most churches look for in a pastor. He was mentally disorganized, an enthusiastic but poor speaker; when he led any meeting he made people feel nervous within ten minutes. Nobody had told him. Instead they had spoken warmly about his calling and had pretended to be delighted at his direction.
>
> They flattered him. I feel quite sure that in private, away from his ears, people discussed him, but they were never frank with him. He might have been steered into another kind of ministry for which he was admirably suited, but nobody wanted to pop his bubble. Instead they set 'a net for his feet'.
>
> In the end he was devastated. He had spent years of his life, going in a direction that was from the beginning almost bound to be fruitless.[3]

Whether our motives are good or not, the result of flattery is the same. If those around us shield us from a realistic understanding of our strengths and weaknesses, they are not showing real love or being good friends. Not only can this lead to failure and disappointment, as in the tragic case of that would-be pastor; we can also be deceived into disregarding the very sin or weakness that disables our walk with God. Those who say the nicest things are not always the best friends.

Some of my most valued friends are people I initially found difficult to get on with. They weren't easy on the ear; they asked searching questions, making me feel uncomfortable. Their example and observations caused me to examine areas of my life. They offered words of praise too, but they were spread sparingly. Others were far more accommodating; they were quick to compliment, full of praise, and I was left feeling on top of the world. But it wasn't long before I discovered who stimulated my spiritual growth, and who gave me an elevated sense of my own importance. Those who said the nicest things, though they would claim to be real friends, were actually enemies of spiritual progress. Those who loved me enough to say the hard things were showing real friendship. They are also the people who have remained steadfast through thick and thin.

As C. H. Spurgeon once said, 'flattery and friendship never go together'. As we build quality friendships, we need people around us who love us too much to flatter us. The pleasantness of the sounds is not what counts, but the wisdom of the words.

Good company or bad company?

Like the crackling of thorns under a pot,
so is the laughter of fools.

(Ecclesiastes 7:6)

We have all met the type. They're the life and soul of the party, the jokers in the pack. Life is never boring when they are around. Full of laughs, they make things buzz. They're such good company. Are they? I suppose it all depends on your definition of good company.

The proverb just quoted pictures a cooking-pot. Placed over the fire, water would boil and the food would be prepared for a meal. But try cooking with thorns instead of wood. There would be a great deal of noise as they crackled under the pot, as if excellent progress were being made. Not long till supper! But a close look reveals the truth; the pot isn't boiling. The thorns are making lots of noise, but generating no heat. They are achieving nothing, but doing it extremely impressively.

The crackling of those thorns is like the laughter of fools. The message is clear: we need to look beyond presentation to content. This is true in many areas of life, and not least in our friendships.

Some people are impressive on the surface. They are charming, urbane, witty and educated. They can converse fluently on most subjects; they are gifted raconteurs and appreciative listeners. They are far too sophisticated to be the jokers in the pack, but they would undoubtedly be described as good company. Yet if there is no spiritual depth – if you can find no real substance in what they say – they are not truly good company. They are actually *bad* company, in the sense that too much time in their presence will lead to superficiality.

Don't misunderstand me; I like laughter and fun, and enjoy being with people who have a healthy sense of humour. There is nothing sinful in these things. And certainly not all people who are attractive, charming and socially adept are inevitably shallow. It is true, however, that we live in a world that is hugely presentation-conscious, and will buy the contents if the packaging appeals – a world that prefers people who are charming or good-looking to those who are honest. If that attitude enters our approach to friendships, we are heading for trouble.

People who are quieter and initially less impressive may prove to be far better company in the long run. There is a depth to them; what they lack in presentation they more than make up for in content. As we try to make choices concerning our friends, it's wise to look beyond first impressions. Whether people seem bubbly and fun-filled or quiet and shy, take the time to look deeper. Look for those who have spiritual depth, or at least spiritual hunger. They will be good company on your spiritual journey. Just as bad company corrupts good character, so good company promotes good character.

Think about …

- Gordon MacDonald's five categories of people as they apply to your own closest friends
- spending more time with friends who are concerned for your spiritual growth and welfare
- giving positive input into the life of a friend this week – going beyond superficial chat

Love ... always hopes.

1 Corinthians 13:6–7

Chapter 5
Back to reality

A wonderful thing happened the day the back yard became a patio. A transformation took place, and not just to the back yard. Here's why.

Dad and my big brother were practical; I was ... musical. I held the nails, they held the hammer. I started something, they finished it, or at least showed me how to do it better. And then one day I just didn't start things any more. I had come to terms with the fact that I was not, and never would be, any good at practical projects. The correct response to them was to call Dad or big brother.

Until marriage, that is. I now had a new home, with lots of practical jobs to do, and a wife who looked to me to play my part. It started badly. Prophesying failure, I fulfilled my own prophecies dramatically. Startlingly slanted shelves, large holes in walls and frayed tempers abounded. Jo was patient and encouraging, and had the decency not to laugh in my presence. Slowly, my confidence and competence grew.

Matters came to a head with the patio project. This was

serious stuff. Hundreds of bricks to be dug up, tons of earth to be excavated and a level plot to be prepared for the slabs. Scores of slabs had to be moved by wheelbarrow and layed meticulously. All offers of help were refused, for this had become far more than a DIY project. And I did it!

The moment of truth came as big brother viewed the scene. My casual 'What do you think?' hid tense anticipation.

'You've done a good job there.'

Just six words. He may never know how much they meant to me. It was the beginning of a new era.

I know I will never win any DIY awards. My shelves are still crooked: I still live in fear of the spirit level. But in terms of confidence and self-belief, there has been a radical change, reflected in the discovery of skills that once seemed an impossibility. And the crucial factor? Expectations. In my formative years I descended to the level of the expectations of Dad and big brother. Later, I rose to the expectations of my wife.

The principle is vital. If someone who grew up in a secure, loving home could be so deeply and tangibly affected; if unspoken, maybe subconscious thought expectations could have such an impact; and if all these consequences could be turned around so radically by another set of expectations, then the expectations of others must be a very powerful force in our lives. The more important people are to us, the greater the impact of their expectations of us.

In part, we become what the people closest to us expect us to become. Although we cannot blame others entirely for the choices we make, and the road we take, we should not underestimate the part they play in making us who we are.

As loving friends, we share in the responsibility for

what others become. We have the awesome power to help them maximize their potential, and the power to crush that potential. In realizing that truth, we unlock a tremendous capacity for doing good in friendship. But there are two ways in which our expectations of others can cause problems.

Expecting too much

First, our expectations of what people *should* be are sometimes too great. We make unrealistic demands on them, perhaps because we don't take the trouble to get to know them deeply enough.

Debbie and James needed to talk about their church situation. They were profoundly disappointed with the level of friendship they were experiencing there. They spoke of other church members as being unwelcoming, critical and superficial. They told how they had tried to reach out, only to be ignored or even snubbed. They painted a disturbing picture, and I felt strongly tempted to join in their condemnation of such a church.

But these initial impressions proved to be deceptive. As the conversation went on, it became clear that Debbie and James came to this church with desperate needs, nursing hurts which made them extremely sensitive, and expecting their new fellowship to be the answer to all their problems. They were looking for unconditional love and acceptance, and total, unswerving commitment, wrapped up in infinite wisdom and sensitivity. They found, instead, people like themselves – people who ran out of patience, had different opinions and were often themselves in need of help and support.

Debbie and James were looking to receive *from* others what they could not give *to* others. The root of their disappointment lay much more in their unrealistic expectations than in the shortcomings of any friends. It was not until those expectations had been addressed that they could begin to build satisfactory friendships with real people.

There is a little of Debbie and James in all of us – a curious inconsistency between what we expect of others and what we expect of ourselves. And we seem blind to our double standards.

Church leaders, especially, are often placed on a pedestal. Then, when they fail to live up to our ideals, we criticize them harshly. 'I never expected that sort of behaviour from a Pastor/Elder/Leader/Minister,' we say, losing sight of the fact that ministers are ministers because God gave them certain gifts, not because they are immune to the temptations that befall the rest of us.

Sometimes we expect too much of new Christians, looking for a measure of maturity that we took years to attain. How soon we forget where we came from! We expect too much in our day-to-day relationships, expecting a level of commitment, support, trust and love that we ourselves would find impossible to maintain. And because our expectations are unrealistic, we end up placing intolerable burdens on others, and growing disappointed and frustrated ourselves.

Unrealistic expectations drain the nourishment from the soil in which friendship struggles to grow. Genuine, fulfilling friendship has its roots deep in a realistic view of ourselves and our friends.

> There is not a righteous man on earth
>   who does what is right and never sins.
> Do not pay attention to every word people say,
>   or you may hear your servant cursing you –

> for you know in your heart
> > that many times you yourself have cursed
> > others.

(Ecclesiastes 7:20–22)

It is no coincidence that this statement and this piece of advice are next to each other. They encourage us to be realistic about others – and to take a good look at ourselves. Be realistic! That is what the writer is saying. We are sinful, all of us. So when people fail, don't make such a big fuss about it. You just happened to catch them doing what you yourself have done many times before, if you are honest enough to admit it.

We need to be realistic about others. They are people like us. They struggle with many of the same things, and also things we will never understand. They are better at some things, worse at others – they have good days and bad days. They are sinful people in a sinful world. They will disappoint us and let us down, as we do them. If we try to force our friends to be more than they are in order to win our acceptance, we have no basis for friendship. We will drive them away, for they will never quite make the grade for us.

We need to be realistic about ourselves, too. We have no right to be high and mighty, given what we know to be in our own hearts. How glad we are that others can't see our thoughts, attitudes and motivation! How totally dependent we are on the grace and mercy of God! We who are forgiven much can know true richness in friendship if we try to love others as we would hope to be loved.

Expecting too little

There is a second way in which our expectations of others can cause problems. Our expectations of what people *could* be are sometimes too small.

Some time ago I received a friendly warning from John. It concerned Mark, who had recently joined our church. 'He's a trouble-maker' – that was the essence of the warning. I was puzzled. Mark seemed to be a delightful, godly man with a desire to serve and a large capacity for love. I investigated further, and discovered that the problem had occurred over twenty years ago.

Mark and John, both young and enthusiastic Christians, had attended the same church. Both were a little raw at the edges, and they disagreed strongly over some issue in the church. Mark left, John stayed – and went on to take a key role in church leadership. So did Mark, but in another area of the county. And now he was back in town. His return raised old fears in John. Here was trouble waiting to happen, and it was his duty to warn us.

In those twenty years both men had learned important lessons and had matured as Christians. Both were gifted leaders, used by God. John's fears related to the man Mark used to be, not the man he was now. John had changed a lot in those years, and needed to be reminded that Mark had too.

That situation exemplifies another inconsistency that we all struggle with. Our judgment of others is usually based on their past performance, while our judgment of ourselves is usually based on our future hopes. We see our own failures, but know we can do better. We see how we *used* to be, but have a glimpse of what we could be. It is hard to adopt that same attitude to those around us, but vital to make it a priority.

When friends see the potential in us, and take the time to tell us about it; when they encourage us to develop our gifts, and look beyond our fears and failures; when they see the possibilities and not just the problems, then something very special happens. They help to release that potential, bringing fresh momentum and drive. Their expectations help us to become what we could be. But when they ridicule us, remind us of our shortcomings or confront us with all the problems we face, it's a very different story. We can almost feel the fire going out inside.

And what we need, our friends need too. 'Love ... always hopes,' writes Paul (1 Corinthians 13:6–7). Love doesn't judge by past performance, but by future possibilities. Love looks for the best, and in doing so helps to bring out the best. While encouragement cannot make everyone a brain surgeon, when God is at work the possibilities are enormous.

A young man accosted me at a Christian conference. 'You're responsible for this!' he said.

'For what?' I asked nervously.

As it turned out, there was nothing to worry about. He told me that we had had one brief conversation several years ago, which I could not even remember. But he could, because apparently I had seen his potential and said so. That brief sharing of a vision had helped to set him on the road to his current calling: he had just become an evangelist with a missionary society. As we parted, I felt thrilled, humbled and immensely grateful to God for the way he works.

I had learned an important lesson too. If forgotten conversations with relative strangers could have such an impact, it was time to think more carefully about conversations with friends. Imagine being the cause of someone failing to take a vital step because of my poor expectations and negative input!

What power our expectations can have in friendship! We would be wise to ask God for a Spirit-inspired vision of what those we love could be. Are we prepared to see their possibilities and potential, just as we hope they see ours? If we are, we will become part of the process of unlocking their potential. We will invest in their future, not tie them to their past. Our friendship will change their lives and ours for the better.

Think about ...

- whether you expect too much of those around you
- whether your input might discourage your friends from reaching their full potential
- what you can do to change this

*Beware lest we mistake our prejudices
for our convictions.*

Harry A. Ironside

*Man prefers to believe
what he prefers to be true.*

Francis Bacon

Chapter 6
Celebrate the differences

There is another powerful influence at work on our expectations of others. It deeply affects our friendships. It is all the more potent because we are largely unaware of it. This nebulous force has to do with our social conditioning.

On our journey of life, each of us carries the baggage of our background. That will include our race, culture, class, family, generation and church tradition, among other things. These are perfectly valid and, indeed, valuable elements of who we are. The problem comes when we impose our baggage on those who come from a different background. How does this happen? Take the example of church tradition.

There is great diversity in our churches. Roman Catholic, Anglican and nonconformist, charismatic and non-charismatic; these give us a starting-point. Within each group, denomination and persuasion there are further sub-divisions. Anglicans, for instance, might be 'high', 'low', 'broad', charismatic or non-charismatic.

Then there are varieties within each sub-division.

Each church tradition has its own ways of under-standing what is godly or spiritual, and also what is sinful or worldly. Some of these ideas come from the Bible or from a possible interpretation of it; others do not. In our praise and worship, certain Christians would see en-thusiasm as an indication of spirituality, while others would consider it irreverent. In our prayer life, some would find the use of a lighted candle helpful for periods of quiet meditation; others would see it as a dangerous step towards mysticism. The list of different perspectives could go on indefinitely. Even the clothes we wear, the words we use, and the leisure pursuits we engage in are all conditioned more than we might realize by our church tradition. In Britain, traditions and cultural influences from Asia, the West Indies, Africa and America have also permeated many churches.

Our family traditions, similarly, give us different definitions of acceptable behaviour and of the correct way to perform even everyday tasks. If others disagree with you, they are wrong! You might smile at them condes-cendingly, and allow that there are equally valid ways, but in your heart you will feel that they are misguided.

Add to church and family the further diversity of race, culture, class and generation, and there is all sorts of potential for breakdown of relationships. Churches and communities, friends and families have been divided by ludicrously trivial issues.

Each of us brings this baggage into our relationships. It affects the way we relate to others, the way we view them and the way we judge them. The more we become aware of its effect on our expectations of others, and on theirs of us, the more easily we will be able to form friendships that are based on realism. While much of our tradition will be helpful, valuable and good, it does not belong in the category of absolute truth. Seeing our social conditioning for what it is will help our personal development, and facilitate the development of deeper friendships.

Here are some of the ways we might expect others to fit into our picture of what is right, with all the dangers this brings.

Perfect copies every time

I was stuck behind a car transporter on the motorway. It was full of sophisticated but identical cars. Apart from differences in colour, it was impossible to distinguish between them. They had come off a production line. In some churches, it would be tempting to say the same thing of the members. They talk, pray, worship and dress in remarkably similar ways. Though they may come in slightly different colours, they are very hard to tell apart!

God said 'Let us make man in our image, in our likeness' (Genesis 1:26). But in our desire to see fellow Christians becoming more like God, we can inadvertently try to make them more like us. We filter biblical truth through our own traditions and experience, and insist that those around us accommodate to our interpretation of things.

Friendships are naturally built on shared background, interests and experiences. But if we form deep relationships only with those who confirm our thinking, we become insular. There is no-one around us who can challenge our prejudices or broaden our horizons. The potential hazards of this attitude include narrow-mindedness, intolerance and inflexibility. We become suspicious of others who are different from us. We are moving in ever-decreasing circles, and that is unhealthy.

Diversity in friendship can be tremendously liberating, and is not something to fear. Different perspectives and opinions about biblical truth; different understandings on the practical outworking of that truth in daily life – these can all challenge the accepted wisdom of our small circle and help us to sort out what we really think.

I'm right, you're wrong

Even if we do not try to compel people to be like us, we may still compare them unfavourably with us. Lurking at the back of our minds is a fatally flawed equation: *maturity, wisdom and balance* = *me*. As we converse with people whom we find likeable, enjoyable company and erudite, we might describe them as mature, wise or balanced. What we actually mean is that they agree with us! Those who question our thinking and fail to share our perspectives are more likely to be thought immature, unwise or unbalanced.

If we make ourselves the reference point, the final arbitrator in disparity or conflict, judgmentalism will not be far away. Jesus warned of the dangers of judgmental comparison:

> Do not judge, or you too will be judged. For in the same way as you judge others, you will be judged, and with the measure you use, it will be measured to you.
>
> Why do you look at the speck of sawdust in your brother's eye and pay no attention to the plank in your own eye? How can you say to your brother, 'Let me take the speck out of your eye,' when all the time there is a plank in your own eye? You hypocrite, first take the plank out of your own eye,

and then you will see clearly to remove the speck
from your brother's eye (Matthew 7:1–5).

Comparing ourselves with others has several dangers. It
can incline us to magnify the faults of others while being
blind to our own. It can also be a breeding-ground for
self-righteousness and hypocrisy. Thinking of ourselves as
better than others brings false security; we are insulated
against the Holy Spirit's conviction of sin by our pride.

Kirsty is frustrated at the spiritual coolness of most of
the congregation. While she engages in praise and
worship, prays out loud on every possible occasion and is
always ready with a word or two about what God is doing
in her life, others are not following her example. She is
dismayed by a leadership that can allow this environment
and a membership that can tolerate it. In her enthusiasm
Kirsty dismisses the shy, the downhearted and the
undemonstrative as lacking any spiritual depth. She hints
that some might need to leave the church before any real
progress can be made.

The very temperament that gives Kirsty her spontaneity
also inclines her to impatience and lack of self-discipline.
The youthfulness that gives her vigour has also protected
her from the buffetings of time and circumstance. Many
of those she dismisses as having no spiritual depth have a
long, unseen history with God that they find difficult to
express in words. Kirsty has some valid points and
perspectives, but her hasty judgments and superficial
comparisons make it difficult for her to see her own needs,
and learn from the spiritual journey of others.

Of course, if we condemn Kirsty, we may be falling into
the same trap as she. The way we view others should have
less to do with our personal view of spirituality than with
our heart and motivation before God.

Unwise comparison will close the door to many meaningful and productive relationships. We will gravitate towards those who share our faults and prejudices, and shut out those who could give us a more rounded, challenging and liberating view of holiness and sinfulness.

Control freaks

It is tempting to try to control those who do not fit in with our identikit picture of a Christian. We can pressurize them to conform to our expectations, not by persuading them to become like us, but by making it awkward for them to be themselves.

Colin belongs to a church where the norm is attendance twice on Sunday and once on Wednesday night. Many who follow this pattern do so as part of their commitment to God. But if it becomes regarded as the criterion of true spirituality, failure to adhere to it casts doubt on that commitment. This has huge consequences.

Colin, who is unable to attend as regularly as this, is put under pressure to shape up. The fact that he has a stressful job, teaches in Sunday school and has three young children is overlooked. His failure to respond brings a growing distance between Colin and the leadership. He could not possibly be considered for key positions of responsibility with such a cavalier attitude to commitment.

Every week, there is the same question: 'Will we see you this Sunday night?', followed by the same disappointed sigh. Sermons on discipleship mention the weekly attendance hat-trick. Finally, fear of alienation causes Colin to give in to their demands – but at what cost to his family and health? We may be disappointed at Colin's capitulation, but only the strongest-minded can withstand such persistent pressure.

I am not trying to discourage regular, committed attendance. Fellowship with other Christians in the local church is one of the chief ways to develop our faith. But it is possible to attend every meeting and have little spirituality. Equally, we may attend spasmodically due to our circumstances and yet have a vibrant faith. When we try to force others to adhere to our definition of spirituality, we place a heavy burden of guilt on them, and hinder the growth of relationships.

The desire to control is in all of us. It can bring feelings of security, but at great cost. Our love of others will be markedly conditional, and their response to us may have less to do with love and more to do with duty or even fear. That is barren ground for friendship to grow in.

If our acceptance of others depends upon their ability to conform to our ideas and expectations, then the possibilities for friendship will be severely limited. We need to free them from the constraints of our expectations, and resist the desire to make them what we want them to be. Then we shall be increasingly enriched by the diversity in the Christian family. We shall accept others and be accepted by them without fear, offering and enjoying real friendship with real people.

Think about ...

- your reactions to differences in others, and what might need to change
- how you can use the differences you see in others as a basis for growth and learning
- exploring differences as a way of resolving any conflicts you may be experiencing in your friendship

*The life which is unexamined
is not worth living.*

Plato

*As iron sharpens iron,
so one man sharpens another.*

Proverbs 27:17

Chapter 7
A safe pair of hands

Recently I received an appointment to attend the 'Well Man' clinic at our local health centre. The idea behind this is that you don't simply visit the centre when you are ill, but have regular checkups as you do with your dentist. The practice nurse then gives you a thorough examination, including blood tests and a routine admonition about not taking enough exercise. The outcome of this encounter was that although I had arrived feeling perfectly fit, I left with high blood pressure and sundry doubts hanging over my future prospects. My resolution following this trauma was on no account to go to the 'Well Man' clinic again.

The truth is that my visit did not cause the problems, it simply presented an opportunity for them to be brought out into the open. Facing up to facts was the first step in a return to real health. The way we feel and the way we really are can be so different. We can grow so accustomed to our health problems that we don't see them any more. We can refuse to address them for fear of what we may find. And though we may keep the unpleasant reality at bay for a time, it will surface eventually, and quite possibly as a crisis. Despite resenting the intrusion of regular checkups, we know they are ultimately for our own good. They protect us, warn us, help us function well. The benefits far outweigh the pain – if only we would face up to the pain.

In the same way, we sometimes need a friend to give us an emotional and spiritual checkup, to ask a few hard questions. That will mean opening up to one or two very carefully chosen trusted, loyal confidants who are not afraid to speak the truth. It will mean giving them the right to question and appraise. It will mean listening to their advice and (even) criticism. This does not mean inviting meddling or nosiness, or any sort of legalistic tribunal. This is why it is important that the context for such accountability is loving friendship. Friends who can be a sounding board, a guard from danger. Friends who can help identify weaknesses and blind spots, who can help bring wisdom and perspective where it may be lacking.

Your reaction may well be similar to mine after my visit to the 'Well Man' clinic. It is natural to resent the intrusion, and shy away from the pain of facing up to problems and weaknesses. But the benefits are enormous, for we are being protected from danger and guided towards spiritual growth and health. Too much independence can be hazardous to our spiritual and emotional health, whatever the spirit of the age might indicate, and accountability is both wise and biblical. It is also a key environment in which friendships grow and we grow individually in our walk with God. Mary Ellen Ashcroft puts it this way:

Without the help of others, we are like the blind

men and the elephant, captives to our own limited perspective. Human beings have an almost infinite capacity for self-deception. The rich man in Jesus' parable has such good crops that he tears down his barns and builds bigger ones. He says to his soul, 'Soul, you have ample goods laid up for many years; relax, eat, drink, be merry.' What we see here is the individual's capacity to be just plain wrong. God says to him, 'You fool! This very night your life is being demanded of you' (Luke 12:13–21).

This rich man needed friends to whom he was accountable: 'George, I'm going to be frank with you. You don't need bigger barns. You need to give the surplus away.' Or perhaps a spiritual director: 'George, let me tell you something you may or may not want to hear. You need to start doing things to feed your soul. What's it going to be?' The rich man needed the support and vision of others so that he couldn't give himself a warped vision of reality. We all need people in our lives who know the worst and love us anyway.[1]

How does it work?

For years my understanding of accountability was limited. It was clear from the Bible that we are all accountable to God (Matthew 12:35; Romans 14:10b–12). Also that we are accountable to our spiritual leaders (1 Corinthians 16:13–18; Hebrews 13:17). But that had the feel of being summoned to the headmaster's study for an interrogation. However, things changed radically after I married Jo. Living in such close proximity to someone meant that certain character flaws, previously submerged, began to surface. What is worse, they were almost entirely in me. Now Jo loves me too much to see my spiritual potential wasted through sin and weakness. Gently, lovingly, she chipped away at those attitude problems and inconsistencies. Gradually she addressed the laziness, the carelessness, the selfishness. She challenged me to live as a true follower of Christ, not just on the surface, but deep down to the very core; and how I hated it!

There was such a strong temptation to hide away, to be defensive, to deny, to justify, to resent such painful scrutiny. I couldn't even fight back with a comparison of Jo's lifestyle; there was no contest. The only thing left to do was sulk. Then it slowly dawned on me that Jo really loved me and was concerned for my good. She loved and accepted me for who I was, and was prayerfully committed to seeing me fulfil my potential. I could either give her permission to help me by granting access to those dark corners of my life, or shut down the channels of communication and run the risk of being spiritually stunted. There was nothing to lose, nothing to fear and everything to gain.

What I once resented, then allowed, is now welcomed. The years have only served to confirm the importance of accountability and the principle has widened in its application. Friends who form the church leadership team operate on a basis of mutual accountability. A close friend and weekly prayer partner fulfils a similar role on a more personal level. Others do so as a natural part of our ongoing friendship. Their input helps protect, guide and encourage. Without it I would be less than I am, and I can only thank God for the blessing they have brought into my life.

Though marriage can provide an excellent environment for accountability, it has limitations too. Mary Ellen

Ashcroft explains further, using her own marriage as an example:

> At its best, marriage creates a space where growth can happen: growth through encouragement, security and challenge. But it can also be a place where partners provide unhealthy protection and enable each other's neuroses and anxieties, instead of challenging each other to grow. And there are areas of my life where Ernie will never challenge me, because they are areas that he's not much aware of or perhaps too close to. I need others to be mutually accountable to.[2]

It may be helpful to ask ourselves if we have a good, caring friendship which both parties have helped develop which might already form the context for accountability. That means you are prepared to give input, where appropriate, as well as receive it. It implies a sense of responsibility for each other's welfare. It probably means you will be of the same sex. There will be times when the level of input is not the same for both friends, due to differences in circumstances, maturity or wisdom. However, the willingness to make accountability mutually beneficial is an important part of ensuring that it is a rich and rewarding experience. Many who have initially thought of themselves as 'senior partners' in a friendship have come to value the input they receive from their friend more than they could ever have hoped or imagined. But we need to create an environment where such input can thrive.

One of the simplest ways to encourage mutual accountability in a friendship is to agree to meet for prayer with one or two friends on a weekly basis. As trust develops through praying for each other and for wider issues, then an element of accountability will naturally enter in, if you are at all open. The simple pressure of having to report your progress next week is also a most helpful stimulus! Behaviour that is observed tends to improve – ask any teacher or employer. Likewise the gentle external motivation that comes from accountability will often achieve what internal motivation will never do. The price we pay is our pride and selfishness; the rewards are huge.

It may be that even as you read, thoughts of accountability evoke feelings that are too much like a doctor's surgery, and not enough like a comfortable chair and a close friendship. If that is the case, think again. I am most emphatically not talking about a clinical, removed element in our relationships called accountability, where warmth and love are replaced by inquisition and criticism. A much better understanding is of accountability being a natural part of our friendship; an openness that is a response to being in a safe place, where questions are asked out of deep love and concern for our best.

If we want to know the blessing of deeper friendships and a deeper spiritual life, then accountability will play a vital part. It is a conscious choice we make to invite others into our lives, and also to care enough about others to ask them the hard questions. The benefits far outweigh the pain – if only we will face up to the pain.

Ask yourself …

- Do any of your friends feel free to drop in or telephone you without a specific reason?
- Does anyone outside your family feel free to question your actions if they seem unwise or hurtful?
- Do you ever discuss private matters such as your

money, work practices or sexual temptation with your friends?

Think about ...

- whether you need to take action to become more accountable to others
- whom you know who could fulfil that role in your life

And maybe even ...

- make a 'hit list' of those you might ask to help you be accountable
- form a prayer triplet

They never taste who always drink;
they always talk who never think.

Matthew Prior

Where words are many, sin is not absent,
but he who hold his tongue is wise.

Proverbs 10:19

Chapter 8
Breaking down the barriers

Much technological innovation focuses on the development of better communication networks. Efficient communication is deemed vital in the expansion of businesses and the evolution of commercial partnerships. Speed of communication in the global village is of little value, however, unless the message is intelligible and of interest; hence the plethora of courses designed to develop communication skills. Clear, concise, winsome speech, writing or multimedia presentation is considered essential to building good business relationships.

Sadly, so little of the time, energy and expertise devoted to nourishing business relationships spills over into developing of good interpersonal relationships. Take Greg, for instance. Greg runs a successful advertising company. He is stimulating and highly articulate in winning new contracts, and clients find him excellent company. But that is not the experience of those closest to him. Greg is often curt with his staff and monosyllabic with his wife. He can see the return on his investment in business terms, as the contracts roll in and the client-base flourishes. He fails to see the damage his lack of investment is causing in loss of loyalty and of love, and in failure to develop any meaningful relationships.

If we are to build quality friendships, our ability to communicate more than superficially is essential. This is not simply a matter of skill and technique; love and commitment are a major part of the equation. Humility, openness and trust are important in fostering good communication between people. This will in turn help friendship to grow and prosper.

Humility: nothing to prove

All of you, clothe yourselves with humility toward one another, because,

'God opposes the proud
but gives grace to the humble.'

(1 Peter 5:5)

Love ... does not boast, it is not proud.

(1 Corinthians 13:4)

The essence of sin is pride. It keeps us from submitting our will to God. It consumes our thinking, and poisons our relationships. Pride is concerned with excelling over others, and is thus competitive. Our preoccupation with self leads us to ignore, use or even humiliate others. God hates pride; it is one of the few things that he despises (Proverbs 8:13).

Pride ruins friendships. If we cannot face up to our weaknesses and needs, our friendships will be dogged by shallowness and lack of reality. If we cannot admit our faults and wrongdoing, our friendships will break down whenever there is conflict. The first step towards dealing with pride is to acknowledge that we are proud. Though that would seem obvious, it is not always easy, as one of the primary symptoms of pride is self-deception. It takes an openness to the Holy Spirit's convicting power to begin that process.

The second step involves 'clothing ourselves' with humility. This is a conscious decision to act against our fallen nature. It is important to understand what is meant by 'humility'. Richard Foster says:

> Put in simple terms, humility means to live as close to the truth as possible: the truth about ourselves, the truth about others, the truth about the world in which we live ... It does not mean grovelling, or finding the worst possible things to say about ourselves.[1]

The word 'humility' comes from the Latin *humus*, which means 'fertile ground'. There is truly no more fertile ground for our faith to grow in, or for our friendships to flourish in than humility. Francis Frangipane graphically impresses upon us its power:

> Satan fears virtue. He is terrified of humility; he hates it. He sees a humble person and it sends chills down his back. His hair stands up when Christians kneel down, for humility is the surrender of the soul to God. The devil trembles before the meek, because in the very areas where he once had access, there stands the Lord, and Satan is terrified of Jesus Christ.[2]

Some people exhibit an apparent humility as a sign of their spirituality. This is often pride masquerading as humility. It can be distinguished from the real thing by studying their openness to input from others. As Virgil Vogt once said, 'If you cannot listen to your brother, you cannot listen to the Holy Spirit.'

Humility opens wide the door which pride keeps closed. Humble people have nothing to prove and nothing to hide. They do not secretly delight in the downfall of another, for their self-esteem is not derived from comparing themselves with others. Humility is the soil in which other qualities essential to good communication can grow.

Openness: nothing to hide

Psychiatrist Robin Skynner has written about studies carried out in America and Britain which focus on individuals and families considered mentally healthy. These are people highly valued by their community and positive in their attitude to life and to others. They seem to enjoy themselves and each other. Particularly striking is the fact that they reach out and are friendly and open with the people around them. This attitude draws a positive response; others cannot help reciprocating with warmth and friendliness.

This refreshing attitude does not stem from unhealthy optimism. The studies showed that such people are in fact very realistic, as Skynner makes clear:

> They know people can be good and bad, so they're not easily deceived. But they accept people as they are, taking the rough with the smooth. And they'll tend to give the benefit of the doubt to people who

appear unfriendly at first. They'll reach out to
strangers in an open and accepting way and won't
immediately withdraw if they don't get a warm
response back. [3]

This attitude stems in part from a sense of personal
security and self-worth, but there is also a sense of wanting
to share with others out of their plenty. It is the same sort
of attitude that we should try to display as we reach out to
others. Whatever our family background, our adoption
into God's family brings an unshakeable basis for security
and self-worth, and the plenty from which we share is
inexhaustible. That is not to deny or devalue the effects of
our past experiences. It is simply to point to the source of
our healing and redemption, and the possibilities inherent
in our new life as Christians.

Openness *with* others means that we are willing to
give of ourselves. We will try to share honestly, not being
constantly on the defensive. We will candidly admit to our
shortcomings, not just to our achievements. We will talk
about our feelings, not shy away from anything personal.
Openness *to* others means that we are willing to receive
from them. We will be concerned about the feelings of
those around us, and receive their confidences as valued
expressions of a growing friendship. We will receive
their admissions of weakness as precious indications of
increasing trust. Furthermore, we will accept their input
and advice as tangible evidence of their developing care
and concern.

An attitude of openness helps friendship to begin,
encourages it to grow, and causes it to endure. It is a fruit
of humility, and a telling weapon against pride.

Trust: nothing to fear

Of course, openness can be abused, which takes us to the next quality we need in true friendship: trust. The very reason many people are defensive and slow to share themselves is that they have trusted others and been hurt in the process. Their confidences have been broken, their fragile emotions have become public knowledge and their innermost thoughts have been passed on as an entertaining diversion. Friendship should be a safe place, and trust helps make it so.

Sue and Tim had been coming to our church for some time. They seemed very much at home and appreciative of all that was going on. Yet whenever they were given the opportunity to get more involved they took a step back. One evening they came round for a meal and explained why. Both gifted individuals, they had thrown themselves into their previous local church with enthusiasm. They gradually got to know the leadership team and opened up about their struggles and fears as well as their hopes and dreams, feeling that this was indeed a safe place. One leader shared this information with his wife; she in turn leaked confidential information to some friends. It wasn't long before a distorted version of Tim's and Sue's closest secrets became a matter for public consumption and opinion. They left the church feeling confused, embarrassed and betrayed, and determined never to give anyone the opportunity to abuse them in this way again.

Our conversation began a long process of healing damage that had taken only minutes to inflict.

Most of what the Bible has to say about gossip is found in the book of Proverbs. Here are two examples. 'A gossip betrays a confidence, but a trustworthy man keeps a secret' (11:13). 'A gossip betrays a confidence, so avoid a man who talks too much' (20:19). Perhaps you have a picture in your mind of what gossips are like. They may be on the phone sharing the latest juicy morsel with a friend, or whispering in corners with conspirators. They are always trying to winkle out the latest news, and people avoid them whenever possible. Such caricatures are unhelpful, however, for they exclude most gossips, who operate on a more subtle and sophisticated level.

A gossip is someone who betrays a confidence. Nothing more, nothing less. It doesn't matter how we dress it up: if we cannot keep secrets, we are not trustworthy; we are gossips. In the Christian community it is all too easy to 'share' what we have heard with a few trusted friends. We value their wisdom and perspective; we know they will pray. That is our excuse, anyway. In this way, half the church has come to know someone's secret, and I wonder how many of them are truly praying. If another friend did the same to us, we would be devastated, but, if they did, they would only be following our example.

Trust concerns far more than keeping secrets. Many things shared in the security of friendship are simply not for wider consumption. They are private. It might be those hopes and dreams for the future that our friends hardly dare express; it could be those fears and insecurities that they are embarrassed to verbalize. They are too precious, too fragile to merit public analysis. To publicize them would be inappropriate, unhelpful and cruel. If we cannot be trusted with such valuable treasures, we will find it hard to maintain good friendships.

Those interesting people who can always give you the latest gossip about everyone else will be equally happy to talk to others about you. Other friends may not seem so interesting; they never seem to have any titbits of information. Perhaps that is because they are trustworthy, not because they are dull. Friendships will not grow where there is no trust. Fear and scepticism will always stunt them. If we look for friends who can be trusted, and behave trustworthily ourselves, communication can be open and free and without misgivings.

A good friend is a good listener

'That's enough about you; let's talk about me.' This quotation, attributed to an unnamed actress in dialogue with an ardent admirer, expresses the reality of many conversations. They can become little more than a trade-off between two people: 'If I listen to her, she'll listen to me.' Listening is reduced to watching out for the next pause so we can start talking again. Sometimes we do this because we are lonely; sometimes, sadly, because we believe our contribution to be more significant than that of the other person. The Bible equates such an attitude with foolishness. 'A fool finds no pleasure in understanding, but delights in airing his own opinions' (Proverbs 18:2). Conversation that does not include genuine listening will militate against deep friendship.

Listening requires patience, concentration and commitment. Quick and easy replies are often of little value, and leave the recipient feeling misunderstood and undervalued. 'He who answers before listening – that is his folly and his shame' (Proverbs 18:13). We need to take time, to listen between the lines and to get the whole story, before we can give an apt response. We Christians seem to have an overwhelming urge to give others the benefit of our experience. If our friends were looking for help that consisted of no more than a popular Bible verse, or simple advice, they would have found it themselves. Most problems are more complex than that, so people need sympathy, encouragement and understanding rather than simplistic counsel.

Many friendships have been stunted by inappropriate responses based on careless listening. People don't care how much we know until they know how much we care. Telling them we know how they feel when we don't; recounting how a similar thing happened to us; comparing our week to theirs to let them know things aren't so bad really – these responses show a lack of care and an inability to listen. Even if our counsel is good, our lack of compassion devalues it and renders it hard to receive.

Without listening, there is no real conversation. Here are two important questions to consider during a conversation.

- Do I keep interrupting this person?

- Can I remember what he or she has just said?

If you constantly interrupt and find it difficult to remember what the other person has said, then although you are talking you probably aren't having a proper conversation. Good listening is interactive, not passive. It requires effort, concentration and skill. Here are a few simple things you can do to develop your listening skills.

Ask questions

We sometimes think we understand what the other person is saying, only to discover later that we did not. Asking questions helps us to clarify what we are hearing. For instance, we could ask, 'I guess that must have made you feel pretty angry?' or 'Are you saying you don't feel there is any hope?' Another important function of questions is to draw out those who are struggling to express themselves. The use of questions that need a fuller answer than 'Yes' or 'No' is invaluable here, for instance: 'How did you feel about what happened?' or 'What do you think about that?' Judicious use of questions can communicate genuine warmth and concern far more effectively than much talking.

Give undivided attention

It can be a rare and highly rewarding experience to have someone's undivided attention. It communicates that we, and what we have to say, are important. This kind of listening builds bridges of friendship in a powerful manner. It involves concentrating on what the other person says, looking at him or her, and not doing something else at the same time. 'Listening' to someone while playing with the computer, watching the television or listening to a football commentary does little for the other person's self-esteem!

Summarize

Summarizing a conversation as you go along has two functions. First, it shows that we have been listening to what our friend has said; secondly, it helps us to check that we have understood it. A summary might begin: 'Now let me see if I've got this right …' The very act of summarizing helps us to understand and to remember.

Reflect on what has been said

The act of listening can go on far beyond our conversation. If we make it our practice to reflect prayerfully on what we have heard, the consequences can be tremendously positive. It helps us to get out of the habit of trying to find immediate solutions, and gives our friends the sense that we take seriously what they say. We can also receive Spirit-inspired insights that are of much more value than our instant reactions. Knowing that we will be reflecting on our conversation later helps us to listen more effectively too.

Building good friendships will involve opening up the channels of good communication. Humility, openness, trust and the ability to listen all play their part. As we work on these qualities, we will be playing our part in helping friendships to begin, to grow and to stay strong and healthy.

Think about ...

- whether you could be more open with your friends, and what holds you back
- how far friends can trust you with their confidences
- how your friendships could benefit from taking on board the listening skills listed in this chapter

Better is open rebuke
than hidden love.
Wounds from a friend can be trusted,
but an enemy multiplies kisses.

Proverbs 27:5–6

We would rather be ruined by praise
than saved by criticism.

Anon.

Chapter 9
Tough love

A harassed mum struggles with the supermarket trolley and a fractious toddler. At the checkout she cannot find her credit card. As she hunts through pockets, handbag and purse, the child wanders through the automatic doors and out into the car park, with a busy road not far away. People look on in concern, but no-one calls the child or takes him by the hand. There is a screech of brakes, a cry, and then a chilling silence.

Why did no-one try to stop this tragedy? Surely they could see what was happening? 'Well, yes, but we didn't like to interfere. You have to be so careful about even touching children these days – you could end up in court. Anyway, you know how people get upset when others intrude into their affairs. It wasn't our business, and by the time we realized how serious the situation was, it was too late.'

Imagine how incensed you would feel on reading such a report in the local newspaper. If ever a situation called for interference, this was it. This was a time for running, shouting, grabbing, doing *anything* to avert potential disaster. And if it transpired that there was no problem, so be it. The possibility of saving someone from disaster is well worth the risk of an angry reaction.

When friends are potentially heading for disaster, whether physical, spiritual or emotional, we struggle with the same dilemma. Perhaps they need to be warned, challenged or even rebuked. We agree that something must be done; we just don't want to be the ones to do it. That feeling is perfectly understandable; we all like to be liked, and this is a situation that could bring conflict with someone about whom we care deeply. It is all too easy to find excuses: this is the wrong time, we are the wrong people, and if we lose their friendship we will be of no help to them anyway.

Such thinking is not much different from that of the shoppers who watched without helping. We are actually more concerned about events taking an unpleasant turn for ourselves than we are about the dangers awaiting our friend. We want to continue being nice, saying nice things, although this is not in fact the loving thing to do. Love 'is not self-seeking' (1 Corinthians 13:5). Love cares not about what is most comfortable for us, but about what is best for others.

Friends do sometimes need to confront difficult issues with each other. It may be to do with attitudes, decisions and courses of action, or the wrong treatment of others or of ourselves. Our aim is not to criticize or complain, but to keep our friends from danger. Confrontation is never easy, but the following ten tips may help.

1. Keep it private

Public criticism or confrontation is necessary only in the

most extreme circumstances. It embarrasses and humiliates the recipient, and is hardly the act of a loving friend. A private discussion can bring change without the unnecessary shame caused by wider knowledge.

2. Deal with it as soon as possible

The longer we leave it, the harder and more complicated it becomes to confront issues. Time dulls their significance, memories become unreliable, and the impact is lost. If circumstances prevent immediate action, make an appointment to talk as soon as practical.

3. Deal with one issue at a time

It is tempting to take advantage of confrontation to wheel out other grievances that have been gathering dust over the months. Though we may feel the benefit of venting our spleen, we may well only confuse and discourage our friend. If several issues do have to be dealt with on one occasion, then ensure that each is discussed separately and clearly.

4. Don't keep repeating your criticism

For most people a few words of criticism make a far deeper impression than many words of praise. Unless we need to clarify something, there is little need to repeat our criticism. It will already have been heard loud and clear!

5. Deal only with actions that the person can change

If something has been done which cannot be undone, then it is futile to focus on that. To be reminded of failure with no hope of restitution is immensely discouraging. Deal with lessons that can be learned and actions that can be changed. Doing so will offer hope, and facilitate a positive outcome.

6. Separate people from their actions

People do foolish or insensitive things, but that does not mean that they are foolish or insensitive people. They may have done something unacceptable, but that does not mean that we should not love and accept them. Labelling our friends as foolish or unlovable can lead to discouragement and failure. Separating the person from the act enables us to offer love and hope without condoning wrong behaviour.

7. Don't exaggerate

In emphasizing our point, it is all too easy to use words like 'never' and 'always' ('You never listen to what I say!' 'You are always rude to your parents!'). This will make the person feel harshly and unfairly treated. It is also likely to be untrue, and thus, the force of our words is lost. Avoid exaggeration; deal with specifics.

8. Present criticisms as questions or suggestions

You can reduce the person's feelings of tension and embarrassment by offering suggestions rather than issuing orders. 'Maybe a phone call would help' is a lot easier to cope with than 'You must phone immediately', and will probably elicit a more willing response.

9. *Don't apologize afterwards*

In our desire not to sour the relationship it is easy to back-pedal on what we have said. We intimate that the problem is scarcely worth mentioning, and apologize for over-reacting. This only serves to weaken what needed to be said, so that it is not taken seriously. If we are concerned for the growth and development of our friend, this is not a loving act.

10. *Wrap it up in love*

We confront those we love because we care for them and want the best for them. That message needs to come across loud and clear. Because our friend will probably be much more depressed by our criticism than encouraged by our praise, we need to give frequent assurances of our ongoing love and commitment to help allay fears of rejection. Start and finish with love, and add a generous helping of love in the middle too!

I could weep when I think of the number of people who end up careering to disaster for lack of a clear warning. It grieves me to know that many of them have friends who may have been concerned but who remained silent. They didn't see it as their place to interfere; they were waiting for the right time, and, after all, they had been praying. And now they are challenged by that same friend with a broken heart, broken marriage, broken dreams or whatever it may be: 'Why did you never warn me?'

Excuses sound thin in the light of that question. We cannot take responsibility for the choices of others, but we can ensure that they understand the significance of those choices. That may involve tough love, risking uncomfortable reactions to avert potential disasters. Good friends should be prepared for that risk.

'He who rebukes a man will in the end gain more favour than he who has a flattering tongue' (Proverbs 28:23). Friends who want to mature and grow will welcome input, hard though it is. They would rather hear tough words that help to save them than easy words that let them fall and fail. Handled wisely and well, confrontation will help friends to strengthen each other and consolidate the friendship too.

Think about ...

- whether you are avoiding confronting a friend over some important issue that needs to be faced
- which of the ten tips for handling confrontation you particularly need to take to heart
- the ways in which friends have confronted you in the past: what was constructive and what was destructive?

*More people fail for lack of encouragement
than for any other reason.*

Anon.

A compliment is verbal sunshine.

Robert Orbern

*Therefore encourage one another
and build each other up,
just as in fact you are doing.*

1 Thessalonians 5:11

Chapter 10
Water in the desert

The last few days have been a struggle. I have felt, as most pastors feel periodically, a sense of total inadequacy to fulfil my calling. I have found myself wondering why anyone would want to listen to my counsel or preaching, let alone employ me as their pastor. I have felt weak, fatigued and vulnerable. Such discouragement can have an almost paralysing effect on an individual's ministry.

But a letter arrived this morning. It was from some dear friends in the church. They wrote to express their appreciation for the previous Sunday's sermon. They explained how it had affected them and their wider family, and described the difference it had made to their week. The letter ended with an assurance of their specific prayers for our spiritual refreshment, and an expression of their love and commitment to us all as a family.

Those special friends' prayers were answered even as I read the letter. I was able to approach the day with a new sense of purpose and perspective, and the fresh motivation that comes from seeing God at work. In my drought of fatigue, discouragement and low self-esteem, their words came like a refreshing downpour. I felt appreciated and encouraged, and uplifted by their respect for my ministry. They had given me so much by being able to receive from me. I had been well and truly affirmed, and that affirmation has helped to change the course of the entire week ahead.

We all need friends like that, and shall be valued friends ourselves if we develop the gift of affirmation. The elements contained in that lovely letter – appreciation, encouragement, respect and the 'gift' of receiving – help us to do just that.

Appreciation and encouragement

My friends had taken the time to express their appreciation of a sermon. Their explanation helped me to understand what was good and helpful for them, and in turn encouraged me in my labours over the next sermon. All that time and effort really were making a difference!

The Christian community can be guilty of two extremes concerning appreciation and encouragement. The first is the use of empty and insincere compliments. That is flattery. If our words are not genuine, they are meaningless and potentially harmful. The second extreme refuses to express any appreciation or praise for fear of robbing God of the glory due to him. It is right that God should be given the ultimate glory; everything we are and have comes from him alone. It is also true that we can have a tendency to take some of the glory that is his by right. But encouragement of others is nevertheless a scriptural principle.

Paul encouraged the Thessalonian congregation, describing them as 'a model to all the believers in Macedonia and Achaia' (1 Thessalonians 1:7). He expressed his appreciation to Philemon for the love he showed to other Christians (Philemon 5). He called on the Philippians to honour men like Epaphroditus, who risked his life for the work of Christ (Philippians 2:29–30). These are just a few examples of Paul's expressions of appreciation and encouragement.

Some years ago I was preaching away from my home church. As is my custom, I briefly thanked the musicians for playing. The organist's response shocked me. 'That's the first time anyone has thanked me for years,' he said. 'Mind you, they're quick enough to let me know if I've done something wrong.'

He was thoroughly discouraged and weary in serving. Those few words of appreciation, though they were valued, had not come from those closest to him, and had not come soon enough. The damage was done, and I later heard that he had resigned within a few months of our conversation.

We start to take for granted the qualities and gifts of those around us, especially in our closest friendships. Yet our appreciation and encouragement are all the more precious to those who are closest to us. While each person needs to find his or her ultimate value and worth in their relationship with God, we are often the instruments God uses to communicate a sense of these things on a practical level.

Friends grow through appreciation and encouragement; they can be stunted without it. Friendships are strengthened by those same expressions of affirmation, and are weakened without them. If we want to build quality friendships, we will ensure that those we care for know that they are valued. A word, a phone call, a letter – all can mean so much and cost so little.

If we have got out of the habit of encouragement, it is time for a turnaround. Perhaps we simply need to develop the habit. One simple way is to *think* about your friends. Think about their qualities and gifts, their acts of kindness and commitment, and their value to both you and God. Then consider how you can communicate some of those truths in a helpful and appropriate way.

Finally, go ahead and encourage them! You may well be making a more significant impact on their day or week than you might ever imagine. I know, because I received a very special letter this morning, from very special friends.

Respect

> Love ... is not rude (1 Corinthians 13:4–5).

My dear friends also made it clear that they had a real respect for me and my calling as a minister. That sense of being respected is of immense value, and makes us want to live in a way that is worthy of such an opinion. But it is all to easy to take for granted those we value, and so deprive them of that vital sense of self-worth.

It's Lucy's birthday, and she has been given a jumper. She's had her eye on it for some time, and is delighted with such a thoughtful gift. She cherishes it, wearing it only on special occasions, paying close attention to the washing instructions and always folding it carefully after use.

Five years later, Lucy's splendid jumper is a little the worse for wear. The label says 'hand wash', but it is no stranger to the washing machine. Instead of being folded meticulously, it is tossed carelessly on to a chair. It is now deemed good enough only for odd jobs and gardening. In pride of place now is the jumper received on her *last* birthday.

We can treat our friends in a similar fashion. Initially, we value their friendship. We are grateful for their care and concern and appreciative of their wise input, and in turn we are sensitive to their needs too. But, as time goes by, familiarity, while not exactly breeding contempt, certainly breeds complacency.

There is in fact something positive about this. Like that jumper, a friendship that has been 'worn in' is more comfortable. We can put our defences down, and lose the fear of being misunderstood that we can feel with those who are not so close to us. As Ralph Waldo Emerson put it: 'A friend is a person with whom I may be sincere. Before him I may think aloud.' Being able to be ourselves brings great release, and it takes time and familiarity to bring that about.

But there are dangers in our 'well-worn' friendships. We can lose respect, take each other for granted and lose sensitivity. What was once maintained and treated well is now handled carelessly. And when newer, more exciting relationships come along, those who have stood by us can be at best neglected, and at worst discarded. How can we ensure that the comfortable does not turn into the complacent? Here are three aspects of respect that are worth considering.

Respect for what our friends say

As we form friendships and find out about each other, the voyage of discovery is often particularly rewarding. We give each other fresh perspectives and insights and listen with interest and attention; we swap humorous stories and are gratified by each other's responses. It is a stimulating time when both parties feel valued in the contributions they make.

It is not long, however, before the perspectives and insights can lose their freshness, and the anecdotes become all too familiar. At this stage we can begin to show lack of respect for what our friends say. Perhaps we begin to interrupt their stories, or finish their punchlines; maybe we simply switch off when we think we hear the same old tape playing again. Our body language might communicate indifference. The result is a sense of hurt and rejection, and a breakdown of communication and friendship.

It is important to do our friends the courtesy of listening to them, of respecting their words and not presuming that we can always anticipate them. That is what we would hope to receive from them; that is what we should give to them. They may repeat themselves but undoubtedly we do too. And as we all learn and grow spiritually, we will have helpful insights and perspectives to bring no matter how long in the tooth our friendship might be.

If friends feel that their words are respected and valued, they will be more likely to consider carefully what they have to say. Our practice of giving weight to their words will be part of the process of giving their words more weight. What a great investment to make in a friend!

Respect for what our friends do

It is so easy to stop valuing those practical demonstrations of our mutual commitment as friends. What we used to think of as a privilege can come to be seen as a right.

Carolyn babysits for Paul and Liz one evening each week so that they can enjoy some time together. They were profoundly grateful when Carolyn first offered to do this, and told her so. They checked each week to make sure she was free to come, and found small ways of thanking her from time to time – a meal, a book token, some flowers.

But then Paul and Liz got used to this privilege. Instead of checking or asking, they began to presume. Their small tokens of appreciation have become fewer, and if Carolyn is unable to manage a week, they feel disgruntled and let down. Carolyn feels increasingly taken for granted, and what started as a pleasure is now sadly a chore.

Familiarity has degenerated into lack of respect and rudeness, and Paul and Liz need to restore their sense of value and respect for what Carolyn does. Perhaps they should take a few moments to list her input into their lives. Perhaps they need to rediscover the effectiveness of saying 'please' and 'thank you', asking politely and receiving gratefully. Perhaps they need to restore the balance with some token of their appreciation of Carolyn's love and commitment.

Friendships based on respect for what our friends do are more likely to stay in a state of good repair.

Respect for who our friends are

Love is kind (1 Corinthians 13:4).

Each of us has our strengths and weaknesses, our hopes and fears, our little quirks and idiosyncrasies. We bring them to our friendships. Some aspects of our personality we are happy with, while others cause us sadness and embarrassment. Over the course of time, as we are accepted and loved, we may grow more comfortable with who we are. We deal with our problems, make progress and grow more secure as our friendships deepen. We can laugh about things that would once have worried us; when our friends gently tease us we can see our foibles in perspective.

As the months and years roll by, familiarity can lead beyond security to insensitivity. The teasing is not quite so gentle. Issues from the past that should be left alone are dredged up for the sake of amusement; things we are sensitive about are ridden over roughshod. Physical characteristics such as baldness, attractiveness or weight might become objects of fun; or perhaps the delicate emotions surrounding unrequited love or broken relationships are trampled on. Those on the receiving end may laugh along, while feeling hurt and embarrassed inside. They will certainly be less likely to open up in the future, and so the development of the friendship has been impaired.

If we want to maintain good friendships, we will respect our friends for who they are, and treat their vulnerabilities and sensitivities with kindness and gentleness. Such respect helps to create an environment in which security can grow, and can facilitate change and growth.

The gift of receiving

The friends I mentioned at the start of the chapter made me feel valued and affirmed by *receiving* from me. Their letter thanked me for my input into their lives. They allowed me to enjoy giving to them by receiving so graciously.

Friendships thrive on the joy of giving and receiving. Many Christians have experienced the liberating truth that it is more blessed to give than to receive. What can be harder is receiving from others. We don't like to be beholden to them; it may hurt our pride, and receiving certainly does not feel as comfortable as giving. This is particularly true in friendships which began when one person had needs, and the other reached out to help. In these circumstances it is easy to settle into the role of 'helper' and 'helped', and for the 'helper' to resist offers of help or gifts, clinging instead to the dominant role.

When we refuse to receive, we are actually depriving others of pleasure and a sense of worth. One of the greatest gifts we can give is that of allowing others to give to us.

In his book *Applauding the Strugglers*, Jim McGuiggan recounts a story about the novelist Marjorie Byrd. On a visit to her friend in the Western Highlands of Scotland, the two were caught in a gale.

At the height of the fierce storm there was a knock on the door. A family friend, a young lad, severely crippled and drenched to the skin, had walked from the village to check on Mrs MacIntosh. She brought him in to warm by the fire and Marjorie Byrd commented on the howling wind. 'Aren't you afraid?' the boy asked intensely.

The novelist was about to say 'no' when Mrs MacIntosh spoke the words every boy longs to hear. 'Of course we were afraid,' she said, 'but now you're here it's all right because we have a man in the house.' The boy straightened his twisted frame, looked at the two women, and said with a firm voice: 'Well then, I'd best be checking to make sure everything is snug.'

How easy it would have been to devalue that young lad's gift. There was no real need here, nothing he could give them but a love and desire to help. But in valuing his gift and accepting it graciously, Mrs MacIntosh gave him a great deal. We will do the same if we allow our friends to give to us, and do not make it difficult or awkward for them to do so. If pride or self-sufficiency keeps us from receiving, we are actually being selfish; we are rejecting the very offerings that will affirm our friends and deepen our friendships. It is more blessed to give than to receive, but in order to experience the blessing of giving, others need to be prepared to receive. (Incidentally, there is great joy in receiving too!)

Friendships grow when there is mutual affirmation, when friends value each other. Appreciation and encouragement, respect, and the ability to receive – these are all gifts that will help us affirm our friends. A little thought turned into action could help to change the course of their day, week or even life. Good friends pour the water of affirmation on the desert of discouragement.

Think about ...

- how you could show your friends more appreciation and encourage them more
- whether you are taking them for granted, and how you can remedy this
- whether you find it difficult to receive from others, and, if so, why

*Friendship flourishes
at the fountain of forgiveness.*

William A. Ward

Mercy triumphs over judgment!

James 2:13

Chapter 11
The family business

The atmosphere in the emergency church meeting was electric. The church had never had to cope with such a scandal before. One of the leaders had confessed to an adulterous relationship. Members were present who had not been seen for a long time. People had been discussing appropriate punishments for such grave misconduct, and the level of anticipation was high. At last the senior pastor stood, and the room fell silent. How would he deal with this situation? What could he possibly say?

Then they realized that he was close to tears. 'Friends' – his voice was almost a whisper – 'Friends, one of our soldiers has fallen in battle.'

No-one had expected that. Many had come appalled at a trusted leader's behaviour; some had come intent on getting their pound of flesh. The pastor's words shed new light on the situation. Here was a fellow soldier who had fallen. How could he be restored to the fight once more? The meeting took on a very different complexion after those quiet words.

We are in a spiritual battle. We understand the principle, and have heard and probably used those words on many occasions. Yet we still show surprise when there are casualties, and seem ill-equipped to bring healing and restoration. And when the wound appears to be self-inflicted, there is even less motivation to help.

Although the enemy uses many strategies, he strikes at the same points time after time. He wants to damage our relationship with God and with each other. We are constantly being weakened by sin and disunity. God's answer comes through Jesus; it is his grace, mercy and forgiveness that restore us to fellowship with him. He in turn calls us to apply the same solution to our relationships on earth; it is grace, mercy and forgiveness that restore us to fellowship with one another.

Friendships can break down for reasons. If they are not dealt with promptly and wisely, bitter conflict and deep hurt can ensue. Alternatively the initial pain may be so immense that time is needed before the issues can be addressed. A breakdown in relationship with God, too, can have a huge impact on friendships, and the way we handle it can crucially affect our spiritual progress.

The source, seriousness and impact of these broken relationships will vary, but God's commitment to restore them remains the same. If God had not reached out to us, we would never know what it was to be in his family. Restoration is the family business that we are called to join. How can we work towards the restoration of relationships that break down? The next two chapters will look at *reconciliation*, the bringing back together of those who are separated by hurt or disagreement, and the restoration of those whose sin has created a barrier between them and God.

Ruling off

> Love … is not easily angered, it keeps no record of
> wrongs (1 Corinthians 13:4–5).

At the beginning of English or maths lessons in my early years at school, the teacher would shout, 'Exercise books out … pencils and rulers out … now rule off.' 'Now rule off' – that was just about my favourite moment of the day. Above the line were my scribblings and crossings out of yesterday. Above the line were my spelling mistakes and spidery attempts at neat handwriting. Above the line was a reminder of all the shortcomings of the previous day. But below the line … now that was an entirely different matter. Below the line was clean, pristine, full of hope. Below the line represented all my hopes and good intentions. Below the line spoke of a new start, and the possibility of getting it right this time.

I could never have verbalized those thoughts then, but I really believe that 'ruling off' played a significant part in my progress during those formative years. Without that tangible demonstration of a new beginning, my young thoughts might well have been clouded by the errors and mess of yesterday. But that daily act gave me the impetus to look forward in hopeful anticipation.

There are times in all friendships when we need to 'rule off'. It won't neccessarily be easy; we might be itching to carry over mistakes and messes from the previous day, week or month, but we need to draw a line through yesterday and start afresh today. Close friendships have weakened and even died when people have failed to 'rule off' in situations like those we shall look at now.

Hurtful words

It is not unusual for friends to disagree, or for disagreements to get heated. The closer our friendships become, the more barriers come down, and sometimes we let ourselves go in a way that would never happen in lesser relationships.

The tragedy comes when we go too far and valued friendships break down. Both parties have lost control, both have said hurtful and untrue things, maybe with a little exaggeration or a convenient lapse of memory. It should never have happened. Afterwards, we each go through our own post-fight analysis, dwelling on the hurtful nature of what the other person said. 'Perhaps he was never really my friend at all.' 'How could she say such things?' We replay the argument in our minds, adding all those biting comments and sarcastic witticisms that we weren't quick enough to think of before. We gloss over the pain our own words must have caused, and focus on the injustice we consider to have been done to us. As the process continues, our anger hardens like cement.

It is at this point that we need to 'rule off', to draw a line under that disagreement. That will involve acknowledging that we said wrong things, and asking forgiveness, even if we feel more sinned against than sinning. It will mean letting it go, forgetting what the other person said, and determining not to mention it again. We probably won't feel like doing this; it may have to be an act of the will. But if we can take this step, the process of reconciliation will be well on the way. Anger will begin to melt, warmth will start to return, and the frayed edges can grow together, getting stronger than before. Eventually we may be able to discuss whatever it was that caused the original argument, this time in a more tolerant, understanding and forward-looking way.

Misunderstandings

Between the transmitter called the mouth and the receiver called the ears, there is a huge capacity for communication breakdown. Perhaps the signal was unclear, or the receivers weren't working properly, or there was interference between the two, or our mental playback of the message is affected by gaps or distortions. Any of these malfunctions can lead to a serious breakdown in communication, with potentially far-reaching consequences.

Sally agrees to meet Ben at her house on Friday night at 8pm. By 8.30 she is getting impatient and tries to phone him, only to find the line busy. By 9pm she is angry and and worried, and takes a cab to his flat, to discover he has gone out. His flatmates have no idea where he is. By 10pm Sally is at home in bed, furious with Ben and vowing never to see him again. Meanwhile Ben has also waited, tried to phone Sally and eventually gone round to her house to find it empty. On his return, his friends neglect to mention that Sally has called. He bemoans Sally's unreliability and takes refuge in the late-night movie.

A day or two later two angry people encounter each other, both feeling hurt and wronged. Sally clearly remembers Ben saying they would meet at her place; Ben clearly remembers they were to meet at his. If one of them is lying to cover up, and this is a regular pattern of behaviour, it has to be addressed. In most cases like this, however, the problems arise because of mumbled words, cloth ears and bad memories. Accusations are therefore unproductive, and only make matters worse. Going over and over the original conversation is fruitless since nothing can be proved either way. What has happened is a simple misunderstanding. Sally and Ben will never know who was right and who was wrong; what is more important is their friendship. It is time to 'rule off'. This will mean apologizing for any careless speech or inattentive listening, whether or not they believe themselves to be at fault. Having recognized that the breakdown in their relationship is based on a misunderstanding, they can then draw a line under the events surrounding it, and move forward.

Powerful opinions

We all feel strongly about things: what is good and bad taste; what is appropriate and inappropriate behaviour; what is good and bad stewardship of money and resources – these and countless other subjects have fuelled many a robust debate. Because we are dealing with opinions, there will inevitably be differences that cannot easily be resolved. In the Christian community there is also the matter of endeavouring to walk in step with the Holy Spirit. When Christians disagree about how the Holy Spirit is leading, there is a massive potential for raw emotions.

When friends come up against each other's strong opinions, it can feel as if the relationship is under threat. How can we possibly remain close to someone whose thinking is so diametrically opposed to our own? It is easy to allow our differences to drive a wedge between us. The friendship either breaks down entirely, or moves to a more superficial level. Each has tried in vain to convince the other of their stance; what more can be done?

Where can we go from here? We need to realize that we are dealing with opinions, not facts. Different opinions can be equally valid. Facts don't change, opinions can;

facts can be supported by evidence, opinions by their very nature cannot. Sadly, we tend to place our own opinions on the same level as facts, and so we see the disagreement in terms of right and wrong.

If we cannot resolve the conflict, it is time to 'rule off' by agreeing to disagree. In so doing we are recognizing that our opinions are on a lower level of importance than facts. We may need to apologize for our insensitive dealings with our friend, and acknowledge the validity of his or her opinions. There may be middle ground that can accommodate both parties; looking for it will help to restore the affinity that has been weakened.

Several years ago I sat in a church leaders' meeting. The church had to take a decision about the way forward. For several weeks all the leaders but one had been in agreement. Discussion had been heated at times, and some hard things had been said. There had certainly been misunderstanding, and opinions were in complete conflict. It was an unhappy stalemate.

Then the dissenting voice spoke again. He affirmed the wisdom and gifts of the other leaders, and his trust in their decision-making capabilities. In order to move forward, the leadership team should be unanimous, and so this leader chosen to stand with the majority. Moreover, at the next church meeting he stood up to endorse the decision that he had opposed for so long. Here was wisdom and grace at work.

Here was a man who had ruled off. He had drawn a line under hurt, misunderstanding and differing opinions. He had let go of the need to justify himself. Consequently he could move forward, with close bonds strengthened by respect. And he came to be thoroughly convinced that the decision the church had taken was absolutely right – in his opinion, of course!

Mediation

Some disagreements may be so sharp that it is very difficult to see reconciliation as a viable option. Perhaps bitterness and resentment have set in, or no workable compromise can be reached. Maybe the friendship has been deteriorating for some time without this being acknowledged, and the breakdown is simply the end of the process. This can happen in the closest of friendships, and sadly is all too prevalent in that most intimate bond of marriage.

When this happens it is vital to seek outside help, and the sooner the better. I have lost count of the ministers who grieve at broken marriages, and speak of their sense of helplessness. 'If only they had come to me before the relationship had completely broken down, then I could have truly helped them.' But pride keeps many from asking for help before it is too late (humanly speaking), and that applies to broken friendships as well as broken marriages.

For those who are in earnest about reconciliation, wise mediation can be of enormous benefit. Someone who is outside the situation, who is impartial and objective, can often bring a fresh perspective to break the deadlock. They can suggest possible changes or compromises, and their impetus can help get the wheels of reconciliation in motion again.

If we are serious about our friendships and our marriages, we will look for someone to help us by mediation as soon as it becomes obvious that we are making no progress ourselves. The longer the delay, the harder it is, and though we believe that with God nothing is impossible, our inflexibility places us in a very dangerous position. There is little to lose, and much to gain.

If our friendships are to survive on terms worthy of the

name, we need a commitment to reconciliation. Working through breakdowns in relationships will serve to deepen and strengthen friendships immensely, and teach us a good deal about ourselves too. Ruling off and mediation can help the process considerably, but they need an environment created by a desire for unity and reconciliation which only we can provide.

Think about ...

- any of your friendships which are suffering from a breakdown in communication, and what may have brought this about
- what you need to do to start the process of reconciliation moving
- how God's forgiveness of you might motivate you to show forgiveness to anyone who has hurt you

*The Christian army is hugely weakened
by the continuing practice
of shooting its own wounded.*

Anon.

*Brothers, if someone is caught in a sin,
you who are spiritual
should restore him gently.*

Galatians 6:1

Chapter 12
The offer of hope

Not all breakdowns in relationship result from simple misunderstandings or disagreements about opinions. Sometimes they follow a sin against God and other people, and have far-reaching consequences. In the case of an unfaithful partner, for instance, the shockwaves disrupt family, friends, church and community. The shattering of trust, the sense of rejection and the immeasurable hurt are not easily dealt with. Violence, theft, deception, addiction, rejection of faith in God, illicit sexual activity – all have wide repercussions.

How can we be good friends in a situation like this? How can we love the sinner without condoning the sin, and try to assist the process of restoration?

The power of forgiveness

Before we think about practical ways of expressing forgiveness, we need to root our thoughts and actions in certain scriptural and realistic truths.

1. Forgiveness is hard

The author Jim McGuiggan has lived and worked for years in and around Belfast. Since he has grown up with conflict as a way of life, his words concerning forgiveness are worth listening to.

It's only in speech or writing that forgiveness is thought to be cheap. When it comes to practising it, we can find a hundred reasons (good reasons of course!) why we shouldn't forgive. Far removed from actual offences, painful and often repeated offences, we can talk glibly about forgiving. When we have been gouged, or worse, when some much-loved friend or family member has been gouged – when that happens, the words about forgiveness are sometimes dismissed or qualified beyond recognition. This may be understandable, but it underscores the reality we wrestle with in this issue.

Still, we musn't expect badly wounded people to dispense forgiveness the way a cigarette machine dispenses cigarettes. There aren't many things harder to swallow than to watch serious offenders further hurt the ones they've wounded with a (virtual) demand for forgiveness even when the wounded are anguished with the pain. We can't *demand* what can only be a gift of grace! As World War II ended, numerous guards and camp commandants sought forgiveness from those they treated so horrendously and were refused it. Is that really surprising? I'm not saying forgiveness should have been withheld; I just want to make the point that a lot of glib rot is spoken about forgiveness by those who've never suffered at any deeper level at the hands of transgressors.[1]

We need to be realistic about forgiveness. Christians can romanticize forgiveness in the same way that the world romanticizes love. Often, in cases of deep hurt, forgiveness is not the decision of a single moment surrounded by a warm glow. It is a painful battle, where ground is won and lost, and a huge effort of will is required.

2. Forgiveness is essential

The Bible makes it clear that forgiveness is not an optional extra for the Christian. In the model prayer that Jesus taught his disciples are the words: 'Forgive us our sins, for we also forgive everyone who sins against us' (Luke 11:4). We can ask God for forgiveness only when we have first forgiven others.

The point is made even more forcibly in the parable of the unmerciful servant (Matthew 18:21–35). In response to Peter's question about how often he should forgive someone, Jesus tells the story of a king who is settling his accounts. One servant owes a phenomenal amount of money, millions of pounds, which he could never hope to repay. The king is within his rights to sell the servant, his family and all his belongings to help repay the debt. Instead, on hearing the man's pleas for mercy, he cancels the debt completely and lets him go.

The same man is owed a few pounds by a fellow servant. He demands the money back immediately, refuses all entreaties for mercy, and has his fellow servant thrown into prison until the debt can be paid. The other servants are horrified at what they have witnessed, and report back to their master. In response the master sends for the man and rebukes him for his wickedness in being so unmerciful, having been shown such mercy. Finally, in his anger the master insists on justice, handing the unmerciful servant over to the jailers until he could pay back all he owed.

Jesus' conclusion is: 'This is how my heavenly Father will treat each of you unless you forgive your brother from your heart' (Matthew 18:35). The message is clear: how can we, who are totally dependent on God's mercy and forgiveness, withhold mercy and forgiveness from others? There is a powerful connection between us forgiving others and enjoying God's forgiveness ourselves. Paul emphasizes this: 'Be kind and compassionate to one another, forgiving each other, just as God in Christ forgave you' (Ephesians 4:32).

It is difficult to forgive. We feel that those who hurt us do not deserve grace, mercy and forgiveness. But neither do we, and that is precisely what God poured out on us through Jesus. The whole point about grace and mercy is that they are not deserved! It isn't a question of whether people deserve forgiveness, or even whether we feel like forgiving them; we are called, commanded, to forgive. However unpalatable that truth may be, it remains a fundamental of Christian living, and one we must work through if we are serious about our spiritual development.

'But they haven't repented, so how can we forgive them?' This is often our excuse when we are looking for a get-out clause! But Paul writes that 'God demonstrates his own love for us in this: while we were still sinners, Christ died for us' (Romans 5:8). It was not when we repented that Christ died for us. It was right in the middle of our pride, sin and rebellion that God reached out with his grace, mercy and forgiveness. And Jesus is our example. Without repentance there cannot be restoration, but there can be forgiveness. It is hard, it is costly, but it is also essential.

We now look at three ways in which we can demonstrate forgiveness.

1. Minimize the impact of sin

> He who covers over an offence promotes love,
>> but whoever repeats the matter separates close
>> friends.

(Proverbs 17:9)

One of the proofs that you have forgiven someone is that you don't let other people know what the person did to you (unless, of course, a crime was committed and the authorities must be informed.) Anger and hurt might cause us to want everyone to know what a despicable thing your 'friend' did, but that will do nothing but hinder the process of restoration. It will further drive a wedge between you, and alienate the person from others who might help. Covering over an offence shows true grace and forgiveness, and points the person causing the hurt in the direction of the cross.

This doesn't in any way condone whatever wrong may have been done. It does, however, create a caring environment in which repentance and restoration are made easier. If we have truly forgiven our friend, we want the best for him or her, and that will include providing protection from the consequences of sin wherever possible.

2. Keep the channels of communication open

When we feel hurt by a friend, it is tempting to maintain an icy distance in order to make it plain just how aggrieved we feel. If the friend comes to ask for forgiveness on bended knee, the ice might melt a little, but until then communication is suspended. This tactic is used not only by friends, but sadly by church leaders too at times. It is what I call the 'Little Bo Peep' method of pastoral care. 'Leave them alone, and they'll come home, bringing their tails behind them.' Thus we make the offender suffer.

The problem with this method is that very often they *don't* come home. At a point of great need, they feel rejected by those who preach about love and forgiveness. The door of friendship has been firmly closed, and it is difficult to know where to turn. In their discouragement and disillusionment they are drawn to others who are more accepting, and so drift away from the Christian community.

I am not suggesting that we should try to return instantly to the relationship we had before. Without repentance, that is not possible, and it inevitably takes time for trust to grow again. What we can do is keep the door open: a quiet word, a phone call, or (if that is too painful) a brief note, to express continued care and concern. We may need to say how much we have been hurt, but also to indicate a willingness to be part of the restoration process. Keeping open the channels of communication speaks of the possibility of acceptance, and helps to remove the fear that divides.

3. Balance truth and love

Mercy triumphs over judgment! (James 2:13).

A further indication that we have forgiven someone is that we truly want to see that person restored, and able to forgive himself or herself. Our sense of fair play may want our friend to feel really bad about his or her behaviour for a while, but that does not show a spirit of love and mercy.

Paul talks of two different types of sorrow; 'worldly sorrow', which leads to death, and 'godly sorrow', which 'brings repentance that leads to salvation and leaves no regret' (2 Corinthians 7:10). Regret is a million miles away from repentance, and so are its consequences. We don't want those we love to feel bad about themselves in a way that separates them still further from us and God. We want them to turn away from their sin and find forgiveness. Truth says that sin has been committed, and there is a price to pay. Love points to the one who has paid the price already.

Churches and individuals that are big on proclaiming truth sometimes find it a little harder to demonstrate love. They may be able to dot their doctrinal 'i's and cross their theological 't's. They may well be able to explain to people what they are doing wrong, and what they should be doing right. But when it comes to actually getting alongside them and helping them through the consequences of their sin, that's a different matter. Please don't misunderstand me; it is vital to have the truth. But in our relationships with others, it is no good having the truth without love, or the struggler will be driven to those who have love without the truth.

Some years ago at a Christian conference, I spent some time with a young man (I shall call him Phil) who had long been struggling with his homosexual orientation. He had never committed a homosexual act, but had experienced temptation in that way. Phil summoned great reserves of courage to talk with friends at church and then with the leadership, only to be met with hostility and condemnation. In despair he turned to the local homosexual community, who gave him warmth, understanding and acceptance, telling him that his feelings were completely natural. Step by step, Phil had entered this new world, until he found himself shocked at the depths to which he had sunk. Now he was looking for a new start, a restored relationship with God.

Phil took responsibility for his own actions, but one of his comments that evening was heartbreaking. 'If only my Christian friends had loved me, and helped me work this through, instead of condemning me, this might never have happened.'

If we want to see our friends restored and repentant, rather than full of regret, we will pray for forgiving love. Where there is love, people can receive truth.

The offer of hope

In his book *Rebuilding your Broken World*, Gordon MacDonald recounts a story told by Jane McAdams. Her mother was due to go into hospital with symptoms which suggested serious cancer. It was soon to be her seventieth birthday, and Jane decided to buy her a new nightgown and robe. After opening the gift and studying it for some time, her mother said that she didn't really want the gown and robe, and asked if they could be returned to the store. Instead, she pointed to an expensive designer summer purse (handbag) which was advertised in the paper, and told her amazed daughter that this was what she really wanted. Jane continues the story.

> My reaction was one of disbelief. Why would my mother, so careful about extravagances, want an expensive summer purse in January, one that she could not possibly use until June? She would not even live until spring, let alone summer. Almost immediately, I was ashamed and appalled at my clumsiness, ignorance, insensitivity, call it what you will. With a shock, I realized she was finally asking me what I thought about her illness. She was asking me how long she would live. She was in fact asking me if I thought she would live even six months. And she was telling me that if I showed I believed she would live until then, then she would do it. She would not let that expensive purse go unused. That day I returned the gown and robe and bought the summer purse.
>
> That was many years ago. The purse is worn out and long gone, as are at least half a dozen others. And next week my mother flies to California to celebrate her 83rd birthday. My gift to her? The most expensive designer purse I could find. She'll use it well.

Gordon MacDonald uses this poignant story to emphasize the power of hope in the process of restoration. He goes on to write:

> The gift of restorative grace to a broken-world person is the gift not of a nightgown that announces death but of a summer purse that says there is life after misbehaviour. That is the message of the Cross and the empty tomb. And it must be

the message of the church to the broken-world person.[2]

Many who have fallen into serious sin feel a deep sense of hopelessness. They cannot see how God can ever use them again. They cannot imagine that their friends will ever accept them again. Rather than risk rejection, they will simply disappear and begin a new life. It is all too easy then to develop a harsh protecting shell of cynicism, and the road to restoration becomes increasingly rocky and winding. At this crucial time, friends who can offer hope are invaluable.

Hope doesn't mean being unrealistic. To promise the treasurer who stole church funds that he can resume his financial responsibilities may well be cruel as well as foolish. To intimate that a marriage can return to normal soon after unfaithfulness is unhelpful. But hope looks for a way forward, and is committed to finding one. Hope opens up the first stages of the process that can bring about restoration. For the couple whose marriage has broken down, it may be the offer of a time to talk alone together; for the torn friendship, inclusion in a social event; for the thief, a small display of trust. Hope offers strength to those who are hanging on by their fingernails to the possibility of reconciliation. The removal of hope is devastating.

A woman caught in adultery was brought to Jesus. Having dealt with the Pharisees' hypocrisy, Jesus spoke words of forgiveness to her. He then told her, 'Go now and leave your life of sin' (John 8:11).

Working out exactly what that means in each case we encounter can be highly complicated. Take the man who has had an affair, resulting in the birth of a child: does returning to his family mean neglecting his baby son and deserting the woman for whom he had expressed undying love? Because sin has brought these circumstances about, none of the options will be straightforward. The apparent hopelessness of such situations can be paralysing. Friends can offer hope by helping to work through the practical consequences of doing what is right before God, of leaving their life of sin. Though this can be a lengthy and complicated process, just the prospect of a solution brings hope, and hope fuels the advance towards restoration.

Think about ...

- someone who needs your forgiveness, and how you can best express that forgiveness in practical ways
- the way you react to people when they confide in you about temptations they feel or sins they have fallen into
- how your church responded when a member fell into sin, and what was constructive or destructive about it

True friendship is a plant of slow growth,
and must undergo and withstand
the shocks of adversity
before it is entitled to the appelation.

George Washington

A friend is never known
until a man has need.

John Heywood

A friend loves at all times,
and a brother is born for adversity.

Proverbs 17:17

Love … always perseveres.

1 Corinthians 13:6–7

Chapter 13
When the going gets tough

Emma is suffering from depression. She feels permanently tired, but can't sleep, and has lost interest in food. Some days are relatively good; on other days she weeps uncontrollably, feels overwhelmed by fear, and is unable to answer the telephone or leave the house. There was no obvious reason for the onset of depression, and Emma is left feeling confused, disorientated and isolated. The doctor has prescribed antidepressants, but they take time to work, and in the meantime the side-effects, including nausea and insomnia, only add to her struggles.

But the worst thing of all is the response of her friends. Her boyfriend lasted two weeks into the depression before leaving because he 'couldn't handle her rejection'. Other friends were supportive at first, and full of encouragement and advice. Slowly they dropped away too; they still leave nice messages on the answerphone, but they hardly ever visit. The church leadership came to pray for Emma, and the church continues in prayer. The pastor would love to see her at church, and thinks it would really help her. He doesn't understand that it takes all her energy just to get out of bed.

Emma's friends are going through very mixed emotions. They feel hurt when she refuses to answer the phone or reply to their messages. They feel frustrated at her lack of progress after all the time, effort, prayer and counsel that have been poured into her situation. Above all, they feel helpless and guilty. Their love and commitment are being challenged to the limits. They just don't know how to respond any more.

Friendships will inevitably go through difficult times. Many outside pressures can deeply affect our capacity to give and receive in a committed relationship. When our friends are hit by illness, unemployment, stress, depression, bereavement or marriage problems, they can become unreasonable, unreceptive, unresponsive, rude and downright hurtful. Stung by their rejection, nursing wounded pride and injured feelings, it is all too easy to give up on them just when they need us most.

Friendship is proved during these difficult times. It either grows stronger and more secure, buttressed by clear evidence of love and commitment, or it is shown to be superficial, and starts to crack under the pressure. 'It certainly shows you who your friends are,' we say. We feel let down by those we thought we could rely on, while staunch support may come from the most unexpected sources.

When our friends are under pressure, we need two qualities above all: *faithfulness* and *compassion*.

Faithfulness

> Like a bad tooth or a lame foot
>   is reliance on the unfaithful in times of trouble.
>
> (Proverbs 25:19)

That is the trouble with bad teeth. It is only when you really need them that you are aware of their unreliability. They fulfil their cosmetic function; no-one would have any idea that they were not dependable. Then you take bite, and as soon as any pressure is put on the tooth it is useless. There is no lack of pain, but a distinct lack of bite. A lame foot can be much the same. It may look the same as a healthy foot, until you want to walk. Then it simply will not take your weight. The tooth and the foot do not fulfil their function; that is why they are described as being bad and lame.

The function of a friend in times of trouble is they can be relied upon. Almost anyone can look the part during the easy times. It is when others have to lean on us that the true calibre of our friendship is seen. There are periods in any relationship when we will need to give more than we receive. That may mean listening more than we speak; it may involve encouraging when we receive discouragement and praising when we receive criticism. If we are not prepared for that, the relationship is on shaky ground. Just when our friend needs to lean the hardest, we give way. And whatever words we might use to justify our behaviour, the book of Proverbs calls it 'unfaithfulness'.

Love and faithfulness are enduring themes of the psalmists as they ponder on God's character. We who are made in his image are called upon to be more like him.

Let love and faithfulness never leave you;
bind them around your neck,
write them on the tablet of your heart.
Then you will win favour and a good name
in the sight of God and man.

(Proverbs 3:3–4)

The importance of love and faithfulness could not be more powerfully expressed. We are to carry them with us everywhere we go, and ensure that they are permanently close to our heart. Faithfulness in our dealings with God and each other delights our Creator.

When we talk of someone being unfaithful in the context of marriage, the meaning is clear. One partner has deserted the other in favour of a more attractive alternative. The marriage covenant has been broken and their commitment always to be there has been proved worthless. As friends, we make no solemn covenant on a level with marriage, but the essence of our unfaithfulness is the same. If our friendship is only for better and not for worse, if we move on when confronted by a more attractive alternative, if we are not prepared for the sacrifice involved in lending support – then we are unfaithful.

Faithfulness does not mean having all the answers, or making everything better, nor does it mean getting it right all the time. What it does mean is being there – not walking away as soon as things get tough – and remaining reliable through all the uncertainty. When someone in trouble leans on a faithful friend, that friend may flinch, but will not give way or push the needy one away. Understanding how we can best help a friend through trying times is never easy. Staying faithful is a crucial part of the jigsaw, around which many other parts of the picture will start to become clear.

Compassion

'Compassion' comes from two Latin words, *cum* (with) and *pati* (suffer). There are two elements to the 'suffering with' of compassion: we are moved by the suffering of others; and we get alongside them with the intention of bringing relief. Dr. D. L. Parkyn comments:

> A compassionate response to suffering requires that one be moved by the suffering of the other, act to remove the immediate effects of that suffering, and respond at length to correct the structures which may have given rise to the suffering itself.[1]

Jesus demonstrated and taught compassion. On one occasion, 'When he saw the crowds, he had compassion on them, because they were harassed and helpless, like sheep without a shepherd' (Matthew 9:36). His feelings of compassion found their outworking in action, as he prayed for them, taught them and healed them. In the parable of the good Samaritan, he commends the man who takes pity on the wounded figure by the road: his compassion leads to action, helping to bring healing and recovery. Others, perceived as righteous, godly people, had passed the sufferer by; their apparent piety was of no value whatever to him. He needed immediate, practical help.

How can we show compassion in our friendships? The three stages of compassion mentioned by Dr Parkyn provide us with a useful outline.

1. We are moved by the suffering of another

Being moved by suffering means far more than feeling bad about it. Compassion calls us to 'suffer with', to enter into the suffering of our friend. This goes against our natural inclinations. We shy away from pain; we feel others' pain so lightly and our own so greatly. As William Hazlitt observed: 'The least pain in our little finger gives us more concern and uneasiness, than the destruction of millions of our fellow-beings.'[2] These words have an uncomfortable ring of truth. Compassion challenges us to set aside our selfish interests for the sake of someone we care about, and engage with our friend in his or her pain.

But what is the point of 'suffering with' someone? Isn't it bad enough that my friend feels pain, without me feeling it too? What would it achieve? How could it possibly help? Surely it would be better to stay strong and 'together' for my friend?

These words of Henri Nouwen help us to understand:

> When do we receive real comfort and consolation? Is it when someone teaches us how to think or act? Is it when we receive advice about where to go or what to do? Is it when we hear words of reassurance and hope? Sometimes, perhaps. But what really counts is that in moments of pain and suffering someone stays with us. More important than any particular action or word of advice is the simple presence of someone who cares.
>
> When someone says to us in the midst of a crisis, 'I do not know what to say or what to do, but I want you to realize that I am with you, that I will not leave you alone', we have a friend through whom we can find consolation and comfort ...

Simply being with someone is difficult because it asks of us that we share in the other's vulnerability, enter with him or her into the experience of weakness and powerlessness, become part of uncertainty, and give up control and self-determination. And still, whenever this happens, new strength and new hope is [*sic*] being born.[3]

As we identify in their pain with those we love, we are giving them so much more than sympathy. We are acknowledging the reality and seriousness of the situation, and communicating our commitment to be there through the darkest times. To weep with someone can be worth more than words. 'Suffering with' brings strength and comfort, and removes the sense of isolation.

2. We act to remove the immediate effects of suffering

Suffering may leave a legacy that lasts for weeks, months, even years. Just as the physical scars of injury can be with us for a lifetime, so can the emotional scars left by bereavement, rejection and discouragement. But in the immediate aftermath of such blows, there is much we can do to bring the sufferer a degree of relief.

Both physical and emotional suffering renders people largely unable to help themselves. Even if they can identify their needs, they may not be able to do anything about them. They may ignore offers of practical help, refuse invitations, and fail to respond to the offer of an open home and a listening ear. This may seem like rejection, or a plea for privacy, but in most cases it is just that the sufferer's energy is sapped by their pain. Taking decisions is immensely difficult, and there is no strength to initiate anything.

Compassion in these circumstances will involve concrete actions rather than words. Instead of offering to do the washing, we will call round and pick it up. Rather than giving an open-ended invitation for a meal, we will make a date, and come to fetch our friend. We must not act insensitively, however, and must be wary of seeming intrusive or bossy.

Different situations bring different needs, and we may have to probe gently to find out what they are. Initially they may be practical, such as cooking, cleaning, companionship or babysitting. The bereaved, separated, unemployed or long-term incapacitated might need financial advice or assistance, and friends could help by locating appropriate agencies.

Helping to alleviate the practical concerns and consequences surrounding suffering is a precious act of love and friendship. It may not only eliminate unnecessary suffering, but also clear the way to long-term solutions.

3. We act to bring long-term relief to suffering

The backbone of compassion is perseverance, the sheer stickability and doggedness that refuses to give up, whatever the odds. Perseverance helps to bring friends through the dark tunnel of suffering. To change the metaphor, what is required is not the explosive energy of the sprinter, but the stamina and tenacity of the long-distance runner. Each race comes with its own peculiar challenges; it is our task to help ensure they can be successfully overcome.

An unemployed friend may face hurdles like lack of confidence, daunting interviews, rejection, lack of motivation and debt. A depressed friend may drag herself through long months experimenting with different medications, and the need to regain confidence. A friend with a debilitating illness may have to learn new ways of performing everyday tasks, and come to terms with the limitations his infirmity has imposed on him. People in these situations are having to deal with the unfamiliar and the uncertain. Friends who remain constant and share the load bring the reassurance and security of the familiar and the certain.

Sharing the load could mean many things: accompanying a friend to the Social Security office, helping him or her fill in forms, doing the shopping, being responsible for medication, balancing accounts, looking after children – the list goes on. Those with marriage difficulties might need our help as a mediator, or to research other appropriate sources of counsel. Others might benefit from help with making phone calls and writing letters, discovering what kinds of support are available and looking for the way forward.

The pressures of caring in this way, in addition to our own everyday responsibilities, can be considerable. Our struggling friend may be unable to express gratitude, and at times may seem inordinately demanding. But the joy that comes from giving unconditional love and from seeing hope, confidence and purpose in life return is immense. Friendships forged in adversity have a strength and security that come from the experience of faithfulness and compassion in action. And the friend who has known our commitment in their weakness will be all the more prepared to give to us in our weakness, with a deep understanding of what is required.

When the going gets tough, good friends will demonstrate faithfulness and compassion. If we want to please God and be more like him, we will take notice of his instruction to us: 'Let love and faithfulness never leave you' (Proverbs 3:3).

Think about ...

- times when you have been able to lean on a faithful friend, and times when friends have been able (or unable) to lean on you
- your ability and willingness to suffer with those who suffer
- your stickability in showing practical care for those who cannot (yet) reciprocate

Chapter 14
Friendship and gender

Friendships are as varied as the individuals who form them. Among the many factors that affect the way we relate to others, gender is one of the most important. In this chapter we look at some of the dynamics of same-sex and opposite-sex friendships, and try to provide some guidelines for sustaining and developing relationships wisely and responsibly.

Biblical guidelines

Do not rebuke an older man harshly, but exhort him as if were your father. Treat younger men as brothers, older women as mothers, and younger women as sisters, with absolute purity (1 Timothy 5:1–2).

But among you there must not be even a hint of sexual immorality, or of any kind of impurity, or of greed, because these are improper for God's holy people (Ephesians 5:3).

These verses lay down some of the ground-rules for the way we should treat each other. They remind us of the standards expected of Christians, in a world that is constantly reinforcing a different moral agenda. As God's holy people, we are called to be distinct from the world we live in, and this is bound to shape the way we view and handle our relationships.

Part of the family

The apostle Paul's words to Timothy focus on respect and decency in relationships: we are to treat each other as family. Older men and women should be treated with the respect appropriate for a father or mother. Younger men and women should be regarded as brothers and sisters. Paul adds the words 'with absolute purity'; Timothy must not abuse his position of trust by treating his Christian sisters as objects of sexual desire, any more than he would his real sisters. Regarding younger Christian women as sisters would help him to treat them properly.

The Christian family should be marked by a closeness, love and trust that come from our shared experience of Christ and the work of the Holy Spirit in our lives. That is a tremendous thing, but it has the capacity to be abused. Those who are vulnerable can be taken advantage of; spiritual and emotional bonding can lead to sexual feelings which are at best misplaced. It is vitally important to behave with purity, and to treat others as we should treat our flesh-and-blood family.

God's representatives

Paul reminds the church at Ephesus that we are 'God's holy people', set apart to serve him. The context is a call to live as children of light – to represent all that is good, right and true in a world that is in the grip of darkness and futile thinking. Our lives are to bear witness to the truth we proclaim, and that requires high standards of behaviour. Paul writes of there not being 'even a hint of sexual immorality' among Christians, and that raises an important point. We have a responsibility not only to do what is right, but to be seen to do what is right.

Working out this principle in our friendships is by no means easy. We need a lot of wisdom, and will find that our interpretation of it differs from that of other Christians. It applies not only to opposite-sex friendships; with the rise in both the profile and acceptance of homosexual and lesbian relationships in our society, we need to behave with wisdom in our same-sex friendships too.

God does not give us these guidelines to spoil or limit friendships, but to create a safe environment in which they can flourish. Working them out prayerfully and carefully will protect us from harming ourselves, others and our witness as Christians. Bearing them in mind, we can go on to think about some typical characteristics of same-sex and opposite-sex relationships, and how we can get the best out of each kind of friendship.

Man to man

Simon came to me deeply unhappy. There was considerable friction in his life both at home and at work, and he was on the verge of depression. We talked about the support that good friendship brought in such situations, and Simon mentioned his best friend Carl, his weekly squash partner. On enquiring what advice Carl had given, I was met with a look of horror and amazement. 'Oh, I would never talk to Carl about this – it wouldn't be appropriate!'

As the conversation unfolded, the boundaries of Simon's friendship with Carl were revealed. It was perfectly in order to talk about sport, work, hobbies or even other people's private lives. But any venture into matters personal, spiritual or emotional would be to break the tacit understanding between them. It would complicate matters and probably cause embarrassment and awkwardness. The relationship might take a new and potentially unsatisfactory direction. It was far safer and simpler to stick to their unspoken agreement. Yet that approach had forced Simon to talk to me, a virtual stranger, about deeply personal issues.

It is by no means uncommon for men to have such boundaries in their friendships. Our culture still treats public displays of emotion by men as a sign of weakness, and expects strong men to hide their emotional side. Physical expressions of closeness between men can be social suicide, with accusations of homosexuality a very real fear. Men are taught to compete, to be independent, not to ask for help. To admit need or to ask for help is seen as a sign of weakness. Think of the millions of man-hours wasted every year by numbers of men driving around totally lost, the time that would be saved if only they would stop and ask for directions!

In *Men: A Book for Women*, James Wagenvoord highlighted some macho tendencies that can hinder friendship:

He shall not cry. He shall not display weakness. He

shall not need affection or gentleness or warmth.
He shall comfort but not desire comforting. He
shall be needed but not need. He shall touch but
not be touched. He shall be steel not flesh. He shall
be inviolate in his manhood. He shall stand alone.[1]

Though there has been some progress in the twenty years
since those words were written, many men still struggle
with the same tendencies. It is not only on our car
journeys that we men are reluctant to admit our need of
direction. It will take a conscious effort on our part to
admit our needs and weaknesses. But as we do this, we
discover the particular strength that comes from man-to-
man friendship.

We are still attracted to the non-threatening environment of sports, hobbies, work and current affairs, but they
can be a good starting-point. Often the friendships that
begin on that basis can be the most lasting as they develop.
Men who attend sporting fixtures together over the years
often see the friendship grow in depth. The sense of
camaraderie that began with team colours moves way
beyond that shared loyalty to strong personal commitment. Being able to talk at length about computers,
attacking midfield players or brake horsepower with
unrestrained enthusiasm is part of what makes many men
feel relaxed and secure, and is a valuable expression of who
they are. Team activities can be of similar benefit,
promoting bonding and belonging. It is from such
starting-points that trust and openness can grow.

If we fight the temptation to stay on the superficial
level, those male distinctives can be of great value. We can
apply our sense of teamwork to sharing and solving
problems together. We can channel our sense of com-
petition by encouraging one another to excel in personal

and spiritual growth. The sense of identity that comes from sharing hobbies can carry over into identifying with one another in our different situations.

Woman to woman

Laura flopped down on the settee with a sigh of frustration. 'I haven't had a decent conversation in months,' was her complaint. The reason: five-month-old Matthew. Since his birth, Laura had been sucked into a world of nappies, feeding patterns and sleeping cycles. Though her husband Chris was still able to have perfectly normal conversations with his friends, it seemed that none of Laura's circle of friends was able to talk to her without constant reference to baby Matthew. Her identity had apparently been swallowed up in the new role of motherhood.

Laura's experience will strike a chord in the heart of many a mum. There will obviously be times when friends' conversations centre on those they love and care for, and the practicalities surrounding that care. It can, however, become all-consuming, to the detriment of deepening relationships. It is possible to 'hide' behind our children as we focus on them in a way that keeps us from having to relate to others at a personal level.

Each woman, whether a mum or not, has her own tendencies which work against forming deeper friendships. Sometimes the focus of communication becomes things, not people, centring on homes and gardens, clothes, cooking and weight. Perhaps excessive time is spent on trivia, such as detailed plans for each day or week. Whatever our tendency might be (as men or as women), it is helpful to identify what tends to pull us away from deeper issues, and try to redress the balance. Nevertheless, it does seem that most women have fewer problems than men in communicating feelings and being prepared to identify their own needs and weaknesses. That can provide a strong basis for deep friendships. If conversations gravitate towards deeper issues, a friend's vulnerability can be met with empathy. Women need to get away from the situations that encourage a focus on the mundane; those at home with small children may well value an offer to take them off their hands for a day, so that they can have a change from baby-talk and escape from the chores.

Whatever the pitfalls faced by men and women (and I am mindful of the danger of perpetuating stereotypes), each of us needs to think through our own tendencies in relating to members of the same sex.

Woman to man and vice versa

All of us need intimate relationships. Intimacy can be enjoyed on different levels – intellectual, emotional, physical and sexual. The only level that is forbidden to friendships outside marriage is the sexual one. It sounds so easy, but we all know that relationships with the opposite sex can be a far more complicated matter. Sheena Gillies writes:

> Is it possible to have an open and trusting relationship with a Christian of the opposite sex without any strings attached? Is marriage always the goal in mind or can the friendship be an end in itself? I have put this question to quite a number of men and women. The replies come back as 'yes', 'no' and 'I don't know' in about equal numbers. I would suggest that there are inevitably pressures because of our biological make-up and reaction

mechanisms as well as the pressure of other people's expectations.

So we have to be realistic and impose some limits and safeguards. At some stage in a friendship between a man and a woman, it is very likely that feelings are aroused just because of relative closeness and natural tendencies. But I think that it is possible to have a good friendship once you have cleared the ground and been totally open and honest with each other. However, if you are single and hating it, the chances of your being able to see a man as anything other than a potential mate are probably quite slim![2]

In a culture that is obsessed with sex, and sees sexual intercourse as a natural expression of intimacy in relationships, we need to take special care. Being clear about our boundaries, and honest about our vulnerability and weakness, will be of great help. Even after marriage, we do not lose the capacity to be sexually attracted or attractive to others. Temptation can still rear its head.

While we must be realistic about our sinful nature, there is no need to fear appropriate, enriching friendships with people of the opposite sex. Single people often miss out on the warmth of physical contact with members of the opposite sex due to a degree of paranoia in the Christian community. A hug with an unmarried friend is seen as the first step to marriage, while with a married friend it becomes the first step to adultery. Friends, both married and unmarried, can provide much-needed physical contact in a way that is beneficial and beyond reproach, provided there is a safe environment. People will differ in their understanding of what is or is not acceptable; we must apply biblical principles with wisdom and integrity. As a married man and a pastor, I have had to work these principles out with my wife, and with the church leadership. Pastoral care inevitably involves dealing with emotionally vulnerable people, who could easily form a strong attachment to someone who gives them love and acceptance during difficult times. Hundreds of tragic stories bear witness to the fact that pastors are by no means impervious to such temptation. In my own ministry, I avoid counselling women alone (except perhaps the very elderly). Jo and I would counsel a woman together, expressing love and care within what we consider to be safe boundaries. Others may come to a different conclusion; the point is that we need to think through our response in an informed and prayerful manner.

Spouses should respect the wishes and feelings of their partners in this. If one partner feels uncomfortable about an opposite-sex relationship involving the other, that is something to be taken very seriously. Single friends have other guidelines. One woman has taken the decision never to allow a man to spend the night in her home without a chaperon. Another has a pact with friends that if she is ever sexually attracted to a married friend, she will inform them for prayer and protection. Other friends who have close working relationships with members of the opposite sex make it a priority to get to know their colleagues' partners as well. Whatever conclusions we come to, we should reach them in the light of the biblical principles of holy living and right witness. In this way we can enjoy rich and diverse expressions of friendship within the protection afforded by the limits God sets (and protection is what it is, even when it feels like restriction).

Think about ...

- your own same-sex relationships and the things that you talk about
- your opposite-sex friendships and any changes you may need to make to keep them within biblical parameters
- the implications of the fact that Christian friendships are 'family' relationships

*It's not what you do,
it's the way that you do it
— that's what gets results.*

Author unknown

Conclusion
A high-risk, high-yield investment

We reap what we sow, and in the measure that we sow. This biblical principle holds good for friendship. Without careful and considerable investment of time, love and commitment, we cannot expect our friendships to yield the riches of which they are capable. It is easy to feel disappointed with the quality or quantity of our relationships while paying little heed to the quality or quantity of our investment in them.

What we invest

> Whoever digs a pit may fall into it;
>   whoever breaks through a wall may be bitten by
>   a snake.

(Ecclesiastes 10:8)

Here is a scene straight from the silent movies. A pair of rogues set a trap to catch unsuspecting travellers, but no-one falls victim to their scheme. They give up and move on to fresh skulduggery. Days later, walking idly along the road, they fall into the very trap they had dug themselves. We laugh at their foolishness and at the sense of poetic justice in their demise.

The practical advice about setting traps has a wider application. Malice and vindictiveness have built-in penalties. He who lives by the sword dies by the sword. That can certainly be true in our relationships. If we harm others, or plot our own gain in a way which leads to their loss, we are playing a dangerous game.

Some people enjoy a good gossip. They become expert at extracting confidences, which are then passed on in like-minded company. They add their own judgments and interpretations, exaggerating and embellishing, in a way that denigrates others. They have set a trap, and the victims suffer while the gossips enjoy the fruits of their duplicity. But woe betide the gossips if *they* should ever do something inappropriate, or divulge any personal secrets to their partners in crime! They will receive no better treatment than they gave others. It will be no use complaining; there will be little sympathy for those who are caught in their own trap.

Though we might never be deliberately vindictive, we may well be prone to criticize, to point out the rotten apple and ignore the rest of the healthy crop. This has its own hazards. Just as the demolition of a wall in a hot Middle Eastern country might disturb a venomous snake hiding in a cavity, so the constant chipping away of criticism can result in a fierce backlash. Those who have been hurt once too often are liable to turn on us and unleash emotions that have built up for a long time. We might feel that the reaction was unfair or out of proportion, but really we brought it on ourselves. That danger will always be present as long as we remain in the demolition business.

How we invest

> Whoever quarries stones may be injured by them;
> whoever splits logs may be endangered by them.

> (Ecclesiastes 10:9)

Even if our motives are good, we can still do harm by the way we invest in the lives of others. Not only do we hurt those we intend to help, but we in turn are stung by their reaction to us. Quarrying stones for building and splitting logs to provide warmth and light, both have constructive purposes, but if carried out carelessly they can cause harm. In the same way, lack of sensitivity in dealing with our friends, no matter how good our intentions, can have disastrous consequences.

It isn't just a case of *what* is said, but *how* and *when*. 'If a man loudly blesses his neighbour early in the morning, it will be taken as a curse' (Proverbs 27:14). The words are positive, the attitude is friendly, but the result is a disgruntled neighbour whose rest has been disturbed. Even blessings can do harm, if they come in the wrong way, or at the wrong time. If that cheery fellow had thought a little longer before acting, he could have dispensed the blessing at a time and in a manner which his sleepier friend would have appreciated.

Some people give advice or help in a way that really encourages and motivates. Others give the same advice in a way that leaves you feeling deflated, and determined to do the opposite of what they suggest. As we invest in friendship, a little extra thought about how and when we give our input can save a lot of heartache. We need to pray for wisdom and sensitivity, and to learn from our mistakes. In that way we can bless those we care for without it being taken as a curse. A little wise investment can bring huge dividends; inappropriate investment, no matter how large, will always disappoint.

The long-term approach

Cast your bread upon the waters,
    for after many days you will find it again.
Give portions to seven, yes to eight,
    for you do not know what disaster may come
        upon the land.

(Ecclesiastes 11:1–2)

These words are full of adventure and enthusiasm, fired up by faith and trust. In a world of uncertainty we can be so paralysed by doubt and fear that we never reach our full potential, or release others to do the same.

The call to 'cast your bread upon the waters' is probably a reference to the seaborne corn trade of the time (not an invitation to feed the ducks!). Traders took a considerable risk in sending their corn (from which bread was made) by sea. Ships could be delayed, damaged, even wrecked; distant business partners could prove unreliable or even dishonest, with little fear of redress. Any such business venture would involve substantial trust, and it would be long before the merchant saw a return on the investment. It might be just as he was about to give up that the ship returned, carrying a fresh cargo or bringing payment.

In the same way, our ventures into friendship require faith and trust, and a measure of adventure and enthusiasm. There is a risk that things will go wrong. There is a possibility of failure or abuse. We may wonder if we will ever see the fruit of our labours. But there is also the delight of seeing a rich return on our investment in the form of others who meet our faith, trust, adventure and enthusiasm with theirs. Their friendship makes the risk, the wait and previous disappointments well worth while.

Of course, we can always play it safe, never taking risks, never trusting or being open with others. In that way we will protect ourselves from getting hurt, but at what cost? The same wall that keeps out the bad will keep out the good, and loneliness and superficiality are a dreadful price to pay for this brand of security. The call of these verses is to take a long-term approach, to be prepared for risks. Things might go wrong, but that should not be the determining factor in our decision-making. Rich, rewarding friendships are a high-risk, high-yield investment. They are worth the risk!

Other valued friendships may grow out of our own love and kindness to those who have little to give in return. As we give out of our strength and plenty to those who are weak and low on resources, we may never know how worthwhile an investment we are making, not just for them, but for ourselves. As we extend our kindness beyond the bounds of comfort, giving 'portions to seven', and then one more, and then one more ... God will honour and bless our loving investment.

Inevitably, some will always need to receive from us and never be in a position to give; indeed, we do not give with receiving in mind. But how often those we have cared for in their weakness return to care for us during our difficult times! The bond forged through trials is further strengthened. Their counsel has the touch of reality, and they delight to give to those from whom they have received. When disaster strikes, those 'portions' that we have given out have a way of returning to us in one way or another.

We may be taken advantage of, unappreciated and treated rudely. We may feel exhausted. It would be far easier to leave it to someone else, and to settle for a quiet life. We would have more time, more energy and more control – but we would be impoverished too by our selfishness. We would learn less, receive less and be poorer individuals for our decision to settle for low-risk relationships. The long-term approach looks beyond immediate returns, security and comfort, and we find that the hard work of giving is rewarded with delightful surprises.

And of course, it is not all hard work, but mostly hugely enjoyable. From the secure environment of shared lives and growing trust, we can relax, laugh, joke, be ourselves. Friendship is fun, and life would be very dull without friends.

The Comfort-zone

Some years ago the science fiction TV series *The Twilight Zone* had something of a cult following, and recently it has reappeared on our screens. It dealt with the bizarre world of the unexplained and the unusual. Over eerie music, the narrator would introduce each episode in chilling tones: 'Ladies and gentlemen, you are now entering the Twilight Zone.' He went on to explain the dangers of entering this strange world, so that those who did so would understand the potential consequences of their action. No-one could say that they had not been warned.

In the realm of friendship we need to be warned about *the comfort zone*. It is easy to enter, and has the undeniable attractions of comfort and security. We don't go too deep, or make ourselves too vulnerable, or put ourselves out too much. We are less likely to get hurt or disappointed, less likely to face challenges, less likely to have the order of our lives disturbed. But the dangers are enormous, for we are drawn insidiously into the world of the shallow and immature. The comfort zone has no room for real depth of friendship, or for growth and development, either personally or in our relationships.

'No pain – no gain,' as the slogan goes. If we are going to take seriously the challenge to build quality relationships, we have to move out of the comfort zone. We need to make high-risk, high-yield investments, to sow generously in the hope of a good harvest, to take the long-term view. Whatever the metaphor, the message remains the same. If we progress beyond our fears, doubts and selfishness; if we make ourselves vulnerable; if we risk disappointments as well as enjoying the good times – then and only then will we enter into the full riches that friendship has to offer.

I really believe this. I have known painful experiences in my own friendships, and no doubt there will be more. Nevertheless, I will take the risk again tomorrow, for there is so much more to gain than to lose.

Make a start …

1. Invite a new friend round for a meal this week. Plan to get beyond the superficial in your conversations.

2. Contact someone to say sorry, or start the process of reconciliation in a friendship that has broken down.

3. Take the first steps in beginning a prayer triplet (see pp. 85–86).

4. Which of your friends needs encouragement just now? Send him or her a letter or e-mail, or phone or call round with some encouraging words.

5. Get in touch with a friend you have not seen for some time.

6. Make a move towards someone who has hurt you.

Notes

Introduction

1. R. Weiss, Loneliness: Emotional and Social Isolation (MIT Press, 1973).
2. A. H. Maslow, *Towards a Psychology of Being* (Van Nostrand, New York, 1968).

1. In the beginning

1. D. A. Westberg, article 'Friendship', in D. J. Atkinson *et al.* (eds.), *New Dictionary of Christian Ethics and Pastoral Theology* (Inter-Varsity Press, 1995), p. 398.
2. Romans 6:4–8; 8:17–18; Colossians 2:12.
3. P. Meadows, *Pressure Points* (Kingsway, 1988), p. 51.

2. The enemy's strategy

1. H. J. M. Nouwen, *Reaching Out* (Fount, 1998), p. 9.
2. Nouwen, *Reaching Out*, p. 46.

4. Choosing wisely

1. G. MacDonald, *Restoring your Spiritual Passion* (Highland Books, 1987), p. 71.
2. MacDonald, *Restoring your Spiritual Passion*, pp. 90–91 .
3. T. Stafford, *That's Not What I Meant* (Crossway Books, 1994), pp. 88–89.

7. A safe pair of hands

1. M. E. Ashcroft, *Balancing Act* (Kingsway, 1997), pp. 127–128.
2. Ashcroft, *Balancing Act*, p. 129.

8. Breaking down the barriers

1. R. Foster, *Prayer* (Hodder and Stoughton, 1992), p. 63.
2. F. Frangipane, *The Three Battlegrounds* (New Wine Press, 1994), p. 21.
3. R. Skynner and J. Cleese, *Life and How to Survive it* (Methuen, 1993), pp. 4–5.

10. Water in the desert

1. J. McGuiggan, *Applauding the Strugglers* (Nelson Word Books, 1995), p. 46.

12. The offer of hope

1. J. McGuiggan, *Applauding the Strugglers* (Nelson Word Books, 1995), pp. 171–172.
2. G. MacDonald, *Rebuilding your Broken World* (Highland Books, 1988), pp. 217–218.

13. When the going gets tough

1. D. L. Parkyn, article 'Compassion', in D. J. Atkinson *et al.* (eds.), *New Dictionary of Christian Ethics and Pastoral Theology* (Inter-Varsity

Press, 1995), p. 244.
2. W. Hazlitt, *American Literature – Dr Channing* (*Edinburgh Review*, 1829), p. 50.
3. H. J. M. Nouwen, D. P. McNeil and D. A. Morrison, *Compassion* (Darton, Longman and Todd, 1982), p. 13.

14. Friendship and gender

1. J. Wagenvoord, *Men: A Book for Women* (New York: Avon Books, 1978), p. 165.
2. S. Gillies, *One of Us* (Nelson Word Books, 1978), p. 156.

THE SINGLE ISSUE
AL HSU

Nearly half today's adult population is unmarried. Most churches, however, emphasize marriage and family in a way that leaves many Christian singles feeling like second-class citizens. Although Jesus himself was single, the single state is often regarded as a problem in itself (rather than as *having* problems, as marriage does).

By contrast, *The Single Issue* sets out a positive, biblical view that honours singleness as a status equal to marriage. Avoiding trite advice on how to suffer through the single life, it offers practical insights on key concerns such as sex, celibacy, and the constructive use of solitude – and points the way to a Christian community in which all members are equally valued.

Al Hsu is a promotional writer for a publishing house, and helps to lead the singles group at his church.

Includes an interview with John Stott on singleness

224 pages   *'B' Format*

Inter-Varsity Press